Current
Approaches

Cystic Fibrosis

T David and Nicola H_____ ___ ___

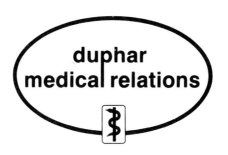

**duphar
medical relations**

First published 1991

ISBN 1-870678-33-8

Printed in Great Britain by
Lyme Regis Printing Company, Lyme Regis, Dorset.

CONTENTS

Editors Foreword: Dr T David

Chairman: Dr T David

EDITOR'S FOREWORD

There can be few diseases where progress has been so rapid, both in relation to identification of the CF gene and the associated rapid expansion of research, and also in the area of new therapeutic approaches in the field of infection and nutrition. This symposium addresses these recent developments and it is hoped that the publication of the papers and the associated discussions will be helpful to doctors and allied professionals involved in the care of children and adults with cystic fibrosis

Dr T J David

THE IMPACT AND APPLICATION OF THE IDENTIFICATION OF THE GENE FOR CYSTIC FIBROSIS

R C Trembath
Paediatric Genetics and Fetal Medicine Unit
Institute of Child Health, London

Cystic Fibrosis (CF) is the most common autosomal recessive disorder amongst Northern European populations, with an estimated incidence of 40 per 100,000 live births[1]. Approximately one person in 25 is a carrier of a mutation within the gene for CF; some 2 million people in the UK alone. By 1985, detailed linkage studies, utilising a large number of multiplex families, had resulted in localisation of the CF gene to chromosome 7[2]. This discovery made available DNA based prenatal diagnosis using material (CVS) obtained within the first trimester of pregnancy. However, such testing was dependent upon tracking a linked DNA probe with the disease, required material to be available from the affected child, and required that there was inherited variation in the DNA sequence such that the probe would reliably distinguish the parental chromosomal 7s; a requirement termed 'informativeness'. However, a number of families requesting prenatal testing remained uninformative, the only fallback being the second trimester Brock test[3], based on estimation of amniotic fluid foetal microvillar intestinal enzyme levels.

Subsequently, segments of DNA progressively closer to the CF gene itself were identified. Using a technique termed chromosome jumping, similar to the widely used chromosome walking procedure, it was possible to isolate a DNA sequence that both mapped to the correct region of chromosome 7 and resulted in RNA transcripts in lung, liver, sweat glands, colon and pancreas, all tissues damaged in CF affected individuals[4].

The CF gene is large, extending over 250Kb (kilobases) of DNA, encoding a mRNA transcript of 6.5Kb. The coding sections of the gene total 24 exons, each separated by an intervening sequence or intron. The mRNA predicts a protein of 1480 amino-acids, called the Cystic Fibrosis Transmembrane conductance Regulator (CFTR) and may belong to a larger family of similar proteins, all being membrane bound transport molecules with ATP binding sites. The altered secretion of chloride ions in particular, with the associated accumulation of viscous secretions both characterise CF clinically, and form the basis of the sweat test. Whether the CFTR is a chloride channel or a regulator of such a channel remains unclear.

The linkage disequilibrium data had predicted that one or only a few mutations of the CFTR gene would account for the majority of CF chromosomes. The cloning of the CFTR also led to the recognition of the most common mutation leading to

CF. The amino-acid, phenylalanine, is deleted at position 508 due to a base pair deletional mutation in the DNA sequence. Whilst in England the deletion of F508 accounts for 75% of CF chromosomes, the frequency differs widely through Europe and in specific racial groups such as Ashkenasi Jews. The other common mutations are shown in table 1. Hence using three separate polymerase chain reactions it is possible to pick up some 85% of CF chromosomes. The reported CFTR mutations tend to show clustering to regions of the protein, such as exons 10 and 11, which form an intracellular component of the CFTR termed the nucleotide binding region. Other regions of the gene are either less prone to mutations, or any mutation within them may not offer the carrier selective advantage assumed to account for the prevalence of other mutations within the CFTR.

The documentation of the genotype for individuals with CF affords an opportunity to seek correlation with the known broad CF phenotype. In one series of 66 patients, a total of 102 (77.2%) of the CF chromosomes had the common F508 mutation. In a further 11 (8.3%), one of three mutations in exon 11 were detected, leaving 19 (14.0%) other CF chromosomes. No difference in the frequency of F508 chromosomes was seen between any of the following clinical manifestations of CF: presentation with meconium ileus, malabsorption or failure to thrive, presence of chronic pulmonary bacterial colonisation or the development of asthma, wheezing or an obstructive defect on spirometry. Similar complications were seen in three children who did not carry F508 on either CF chromosome (R Trembath unpublished observation). Most studies report an association between the F508 mutation and pancreatic insufficiency and at least one group has presented evidence that loci adjacent to that for CF may confer susceptibility for pulmonary complications in adolescent patients[5].

Because mutation detection is not complete, DNA based testing has limited value as a diagnostic tool. The Hardy-Weinberg equation (Figure 1) illustrates the potential for detection of CF affected individuals although the pick-up rate will be greatly influenced by the clinical problem (prior probability) of placing CF in the differential diagnosis.

TABLE 1. South England CFTR mutation
analysis

Mutation	Frequency (%)
F508	78
G551D ⎱	3
G542X ⎬ Exon 11	3
R553X ⎰	1
	85

2

Diagnostic Application

Hardy-Weinberg Equilibruim

$$P^2 \quad + \quad 2pq \quad + \quad q^2 \quad = 1$$

$$\triangle/\triangle \qquad \triangle/CF \qquad CF/CF$$

F508(78%)   61%   34%   5%

Figure 1. Genotypes in CF affected individuals

The impact of cloning the CFTR on genetic counselling for CF is significant. In over 70% of couples, CFTR mutation based prenatal testing is possible, with a degree of accuracy exceeding 99%. A DNA sample does not need to be available and the number of couples at increased risk of an affected offspring with CF, who remain uninformative for the DNA based techniques, is rapidly diminishing. The overlap between family based risk counselling and population based screening also becomes less distinct. The pedigree in Figure 2 indicates the power of the new

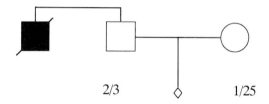

2/3   1/25

Risk for an Affected Child 1/150

Figure 2a. CFTR mutation analysis 'Couple at Risk'

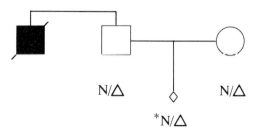

N/△   N/△

*N/△

*Fetus predicted heterozygous (CF carrier)

Figure 2b. CFTR mutation analysis following CFTR mutation analysis and CVS for prenatal diagnosis.

3

technology when applied to a couple requesting prenatal genetic counselling. Firstly, the diagnosis of CF in the brother could not be confirmed by reference to old details as none were available. Secondly, the female partner had no family history of CF and had no prior knowledge of the nature of the condition, its pattern of inheritance or the concept of carrier testing. Following testing, and in the context of a current pregnancy, the need for careful and empathic counselling may be appreciated.

The most immediate outcome of detection of the majority of CFTR mutations is the prospect of population based CF carrier detection. Pilot projects are underway to assess both the potential mechanisms for such a screening programme and the cost (see Table 2). Well over 60 different mutations of the gene for CF have now been reported to the Cystic Fibrosis Genetic Analysis Consortium. However, since the present technology allows the detection of only some 85% of such mutations in the setting of a large scale screening programme, an individual reported as negative for these common mutations will be left with a small 'residual risk' for carrier status (see Table 3). Aspects of clinical genetics like carrier status and residual risk may require increased awareness from a broad group of health care professionals and the public alike.

Prospects of the future
The potential benefits accruing from the identification of the gene for CF and the detection of the most common CF causing mutations within this gene have been

TALBLE 2. Options for population based CF carrier screening.

- Antenatal Clinic
- GP based preconception clinics
- School leavers
- At risk members of CF families

TALBE 3. Impact of CFTR mutation screening

Prior Carrier Risk	Residual Risk F508 (78%)	F508+EXON 11 (85%)
%	%	%
50 (1/2)	18 (1/6)	13 (1/8)
4 (1/25)	1 (1/100)	0.6 (1/160)

outlined. To this, we may add the fundamental basic understanding of the pathophysiology of CF with the hope of improved therapy unfolding in parallel. Coincident with the emergence of such advances in the application of this information for genetic services, is the recognition that substantial investment will be required in the field of health education and awareness, if the goal is providing couples with information and choice in their family planning. Technologically, in order that population based screening may prove to be both more efficient and more widely acceptable, assays for the presence or absence of the mutated CFTR gene will need to be developed. The same is true of the application of mutation analysis as a diagnostic tool. This overlaps with the application of molecular genetics to an ever increasing number of disorders. Therefore we can predict that whatever the spin off for CF, the benefits may find wide application indeed.

REFERENCES

1 Editorial. *Lancet* 1990 **335:** 79-80
2 Wainwright BJ, Scambler PJ, Schmidtke J, *et al.* Localisation of cystic fibrosis locus to human chromosome 7 cen-q22. *Nature* 1985; **318:** 384-5.
3 Brock DJ, Clarke HA, Barron L, Prenatal diagnosis of cystic fibrosis by microvillar enzyme assay on a sequence of 258 pregnancies. *Human Genetics* 1988; **78**: 271-5
4 Riodan JR, Rommens JM, Karem B, *et al.* Identification of the cystic fibrosis gene: cloning and characterisation of complementary DNA. *Science* 1989; **245:** 1066-73.
5 Santis G, Osbourne L, Knight RA, Hodson ME. Linked marker haplotypes and the F508 mutation in adults with mild pulmonary disease and cystic fibrosis. *Lancet* 1990; **335:** 1426-29.

DISCUSSION

Audience Where do you see population screening for cystic fibrosis going? I detected a certain degree of scepticism in what you were saying about other diseases such as thalassaemia and sickle cell anaemia where screening programmes have been instituted successfully.

Dr Trembath I am concerned about the degree of education that is going into the population at large. With reference to thalassaemia and sickle cell anaemia, a lot more effort has gone into those populations who were defined as high risk groups than is being put into educating people about cystic fibrosis. There may be a number of couples whose anxiety is heightened as a result of testing for CF and it is important that provision is made for dealing with that. It is equally appropriate to be aware of the need for education about genetic testing in pregnancy generally, not just confined to CF.

THE CF GENE: IMPLICATIONS FOR DISEASE MECHANISMS AND THERAPEUTIC STRATEGIES

A W Cuthbert

Department of Pharmacology, University of Cambridge

In 1989 the gene responsible for cystic fibrosis (CF) was cloned using reverse genetics[1,3]. It consists of some 250 kilobases made up of 24 exons and coding for a protein of 1480 amino acids. In 70% of CF patients a single codon is lost, corresponding to a loss of phenylalanine in position 508 (ΔF 508). Structural considerations indicate that the protein coded for by the gene (known as CFTR, cystic fibrosis transmembrane conductance regulator) consists of two halves, each containing six transmembrane spanning segments and linked to a consensus sequence for a nucleotide binding fold (NBF). The two halves are joined to a large polar R domain, containing multiple sites for phosphorylation by protein kinase A and protein kinase C. The ΔF 508 deletion occurs in the NBF nearest the N-terminal end of the protein. Over 50 other mutations have now been described which result in changes in CFTR other than ΔF 508. A cluster of four mutations in a 30 base-pair region of exon 11 and coding for part of the NBF have been described[4]. In three instances amino acid substitution is forecast while the fourth mutation causes a termination signal. The consequent changes in CFTR occur in a highly conserved region common to 14 other membrane proteins which bind ATP. The overall picture, therefore, is that the NBF in CFTR is functionally important and that CFTR is a member of a superfamily of ATP dependent transport proteins. Attempts to model the NBF in CFTR have been based on similarity with adenylate kinase[5] but this approach has yet to yield useful information about ATP handling.

The vital question now is how these genetic findings are related to the changes in epithelial ion transport, considered to be the root cause of the disease symptoms. Consider, for example, what is known of the sweat gland and of airway epithelia. In the sweat gland salt secretion in the coil is led by active chloride secretion while in the duct salt is reabsorbed, a process led by active sodium absorption. For a long time the high concentration of salt in CF sweat[6] was thought to result from a failure in the sodium handling process. However, the key observation that the sweat gland duct in CF has a very low chloride conductance[7] explained both the failure to absorb salt and the high transepithelial potential. Thus in the CF sweat duct there is not a failure of the sodium handling processes, but rather an inability of the counter anion to move across the epithelium.

In airway epithelium the position is a little more complex. From a variety of studies, e.g.[8], airways have both sodium-led absorptive processes and chloride-led secretory processes. As the epithelium is water permeable, unlike the sweat gland duct, water follows salt movement. In CF the chloride secretory process fails while the sodium absorptive processes are enhanced (Figure 1). Consequently there is excessive fluid absorption in CF, leading to removal of the sol phase lining the epithelium and the deposition of thick, viscid mucus providing a rich breeding ground for micro-organisms. In the airways the chloride anion which accompanies sodium absorption must pass through pathways which are unavailable for the chloride secretory process.

In the last few years intense interest has focused on the ion channels in CF epithelia, notably channels specific for chloride, sodium and potassium. Sufficient evidence has now accrued to provide an explanation for the macroscopic transporting activity in CF epithelia in terms of channel behaviour.

In human airway epithelia a number of different types of chloride channel have been described, some rectifying and some not, and with different conductances. Channels with conductances of 50 pS (rectifying), 20 pS, 10 pS and 350 pS 7[9-12] have been described and attention has focused initially on the 50 pS, rectifying

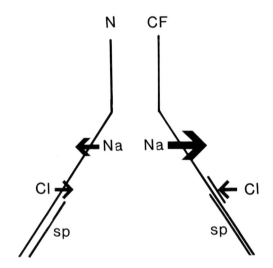

Figure 1. Diagram illustrating the different extents of ion transport in normal (N) and cystic fibrosis (CF) airway epithelia. In CF sodium absorption is enhanced while chloride secretion is prevented. The consequent increase in water movement driven by osmotic forces causes a reduction in the extent of the sol-phase (sp) in CF. Chloride secretion is enhanced in normals by ß-agonists but not in CF epithelia.

channels but latterly on the small, non-rectifying 20 pS channels. (It is also possible that other chloride channels of such low conductance or with such brief open times exist that they cannot be resolved by patch clamping.) However, it is clear that the activation of the 50 pS and 20 pS channels by agonists which increase intracellular cAMP, such as isoprenaline, is absent in CF cells when the recording is made in the cell attached mode[9,10]. After the patch is ripped away from the cell then chloride channel activity can be demonstrated by a variety of means, such as depolarisation of the patch, addition of Ca^{2+} to the cytosolic face or simple waiting long enough. Earlier claims that chloride channels in isolated patches were activated by the catalytic subunit of protein kinase A or C in patches from normal but not CF cells [12,13] now have less impact, as not all agree that the 50 pS channel is crucially relevant in CF[11] and further, isolated patches from CF cells show apparently normal 50 pS chloride channels at 37°C [14,15]. Powerful arguments[14] can be made that the behaviour of chloride channels in CF is determined by the presence of cytosolic inhibitor, which diffuses away once the inside-out isolated patch is formed, especially at 37°C.

Turning to sodium channels, two types of difference have been reported for channels in CF compared with normal airway epithelial cells. Two groups have reported that channel open-time is increased in CF[16,17], while another found that there is an increase in channel number[11]. Both or either of these changes would increase sodium entry into the cells, and provided that the basolateral sodium pumps do not become rate limiting increased sodium transport would result.

Other evidence too, this time from CF sweat glands, points to differences in the behaviour of sodium channels from normal. First, it was found that the affinity of the blocking drug, amiloride, was reduced in CF, and secondly the relationship between sodium concentration and sodium transport was altered[18]. It is possible that the former result is a consequence of the altered membrane potential in CF opposing the entry of amiloride to the channel, or it could reflect altered gating characteristics which are manifested as prolonged open times.

Both airway epithelial cells and sweat gland cells contain maxi-K channels (~230 pS) in their basolateral membranes. These channels are sensitive to $[Ca^{2+}]_i$ and become activated when the intracellular concentration rises by as little as 100 nM. No differences have been reported for these maxi-K channels in either airway epithelial or sweat gland cells when CF tissues are compared with normal ones[10,19,22]. Activation of these channels by agonists which raise $[Ca^{2+}]_i$ may underlie the secretory and absorptive events in airway and sweat gland epithelia by causing apical hyperpolarisation. Recently a small, outwardly rectifying K+ channel insensitive to $[Ca2+]_i$ with an outward slope conductance (+50 mV) of 25 pS and an inward slope conductance (-50 mV) of 10 pS, has been found in CF cells [23]. In *circa* 3000 patches from normal cells this channel has been seen only once. The function of these channels is unclear, but it has been suggested that they may be responsible for the resting membrane potential.

To summarise the results from patch clamp studies, it would seem that the failure of chloride channels in intact cells and the increased open probability of sodium channels, plus perhaps increased number of the latter, do indeed provide a firm basis for the underlying fluxes which lead to excessive drying of airway epithelia.

Recently an alternative way of looking at the changes in chloride permeability has emerged which avoids any controversy in relation to which chloride channels are relevant in CF. Cultured airway cells are loaded with iodide and a fluorescent dye, SPQ. Fluorescence is quenched by halides so that when the bathing solution is changed to one containing nitrate, iodide effluxing from the cell, through chloride channels, leads to an increasing light signal. Single cell imaging techniques are used to follow the fluorescence increase and data from different cells are pooled. Under standard conditions iodide efflux was not different in CF and normal airway cells, however the efflux from isoprenaline-stimulated cells was accelerated in normal but not CF cells. This result confirms that given earlier, namely that cAMP fails to open chloride channels in CF airway epithelial cells. However studies of this type were designed for an entirely different purpose, that is to provide a simple system for complementation studies[24,25]. Molecular biological techniques have been used to construct plasmids containing CFTR cDNA and the ΔF 508 variant which were used to transfect CF airway epithelial cells, so that CFTR protein or the ΔF 508 variant was actually produced within CF cells. Using the fluorescence assay only cells transfected with the CFTR cDNA showed enhanced iodide efflux. Thus the apparent defect in chloride channel regulation in CF cells is corrected by CFTR. It is not yet known whether other electrophysiological properties, such as increased sodium channel open probability, or biochemical characteristics, such as unusual mucus composition[26] are corrected by transfection with CFTR cDNA. Nevertheless the complementation studies do point to a distinct possibility for a genetic strategy for treatment.

However a lot of questions remain to be answered before the functional responsibility of CFTR is discovered. In the final part of this paper some of these questions are posed together with some possible hypotheses for testing. These are: (i) is CFTR an ion channel? (ii) is CFTR one of a superfamily of ATP hydrolysing enzymes such as MDR (p-glycoprotein) proteins or the STE6 gene product in yeasts?[27] (iii) does CFTR have a substrate? and (iv) what are the possibilities of a pharmacological strategy for CF?

Whether CFTR is a chloride channel is not yet finally resolved. In CF there is evidence that CFTR fails to be glycosylated and remains trapped in the Golgi and not transferred to the cell membrane[28]. Assuming this new finding is confirmed for a variety of cells affected in CF, then it is unlikely CFTR is an ion channel, as both Cl^- and Na^+ channels are demonstrable in patches form CF cells. Furthermore the activities of more than one channel are altered in the disease yet CF is a single gene defect. On the other hand it has been shown that plasmids containing the cDNA for CFTR result in the formation of a chloride conductance when introduced into HeLa cells[29]. Normally these cells do not express CFTR and the simplest interpretation is that CFTR is a chloride channel. Alternatively the possibility that CFTR induces activity in nascent chloride channels cannot be eliminated. CFTR certainly has a similarity to the MDR-like proteins but it is not yet clear whether or not the nucleotide binding folds bind ATP or some other nucleotide or indeed whether the nucleotide is hydrolysed. If CFTR acts like an MDR protein it is crucial that the nature of the substrate should be found. The substrate is clearly a prime candidate, as the putative endogenous inhibitor which fails to be cleared from the cell in CF. Furthermore, if a substrate is found a variety of pharmacological tools will arise to alter its rate of formation or catabolism, and which may be able to modify the course of the disease.

How does the basic information given above set the course for new strategies for treatment? Already the possibility of reducing the formation of the substrate for CFTR has been mentioned. Referring back to figure 1 it is obvious that a drug or drugs which could be nebulised into the airways to block sodium channels or open chloride channels would tend to restore normal function. Drugs which block epithelial sodium channels have been known for over two decades[30]. A recent clinical trial[31] with nebulised amiloride, which blocks sodium channels, showed that lung function decreased more slowly when receiving amiloride and, importantly, sputum viscosity returned to normal. The complementation studies, referred to earlier[24,25], indicate that it is possible to repair function, at least *in vitro,* by introducing the gene into the cell, without it being incorporated into the genome. However much effort is necessary before an appropriate vehicle for introducing genetic material safely into man is found. In this connection the availability of transgenic animals with CF will be of crucial importance for testing this approach.

REFERENCES

1 Rommens JM, Iannizzi CM, Kerem B, Drumm ML, Melmer G, Dean M, *et al.* Identification of the cystic fibrosis gene: chromosome walking and jumping. *Science* 1989; **245:** 1059-65.

2 Riordan JR, Rommens JM, Kerem B, Alon N, Rozmahel R, Grzelczak Z, *et al.* Identification of the cystic fibrosis gene: cloning and characterization of complementary DNA. *Science* 1989; **245:** 1066-73.

3 Karem B, Rommens JM, Buchanan JA, Markiewicz D, Cox TK, Chakravarti A, *et al.* Identification of the cystic fibrosis gene: genetic analysis. *Science* 1989; **245:** 1073-80.

4 Cutting GR, Kasch LM, Rosenstein BJ, Zielenski J, Tsui LC, Antonarakis SE, Kazazian HH. A cluster of cystic fibrosis mutations in the first nucleotide-binding fold of the cystic fibrosis conductance regulator protein (see comments). *Nature* 1991; **346:** 366-9.

5   Hyde SC, Emsley P, Hartshorn MJ, Mimmack MM, Gileadi U, Pearce SR, *et al*. Structural model of ATP-binding proteins associated with cystic fibrosis, multidrug resistance and bacterial transport. *Nature* 1990; **346:** 362-5.

6   Di Sant'Agnese PA, Darling GA, Perera GA, Shea E. Abnormal electrolyte compositions of sweat in cystic fibrosis of the pancreas. *Paediatrics* 1953; **12:** 549-563.

7   Quinton PM. Chloride impermeability in cystic fibrosis. *Nature* 1983; **301:** 421-2.

8   Boucher RC, Cotton CU, Gatzy JT, Knowles MR, Yankaskas JR. Evidence for reduced Cl⁻ and increased Na⁺ permeability in cystic fibrosis human primary cell cultures. *J Physiol* 1988; **405:** 77-103.

9   Frizzell RA, Rechkemmer G, Shoemaker RL. Altered regulation of airway epithelial cell chloride channels in cystic fibrosis. *Science* 1986; **233:** 558-60.

10 Welsh MJ, Liedtke CM. Chloride and potassium channels in cystic fibrosis airway epithelia. *Nature* 1986; **322:** 467-70.

11 Duszyk M, French AS, Man SF. Cystic fibrosis affects chloride and sodium channels in human airway epithelia. *Can J Physiol Pharmacol* 1989; **67**(10): 1362-5.

12 Schoumacher RA, Shoemaker RL, Halm DR, Tallant EA, Wallace RW, Frizzell RA. Phosphorylation fails to activate chloride channels from cystic fibrosis airway cells. *Nature* 1978; **330:** 752-4.

13 Hwang TC, Lu L, Zeitlin PL, Gruenert DC, Huganir R, Guggino WB. Cl⁻ channels in CF: lack of activation by protein kinase C and cAMP-dependent protein kinase. *Science* 1989; **244:** 1351-3.

14 Kunzelmann K, Pavenstadt H, Greger R. Properties and regulation of chloride channels in cystic fibrosis and normal airway cells. *Pflugers Arch* 1989; **415:** 172-82.

15 Welsh M J, Li M, McCann JD. Activation of normal and cystic fibrosis Cl⁻ channels by voltage, temperature, and trypsin. *J Clin Invest* 1989; **84:** 2002-7.

16 Disser J, Fromter E. Properties of Na+ channels in respiratory epithelium from CF and non-CF patients. *Pediatr Pulmonol* 1953; Suppl. 4: 115.

17 Chinet Th, Fulton J, Boucher R, Stutts J. Sodium channels in the apical membrane of normal and CF nasal epithelial cells. *Pediatr Pulmonol* 1990; Suppl 5: 209.

18 Cuthbert AW, Brayden DJ, Dunne A, Smyth RL, Wallwork J. Altered sensitivity to amiloride in cystic fibrosis. Observations using cultured sweat glands. *Br J Clin Pharmacol* 1990; **29**: 227-34.

19 Kunzelmann K, Pavenstadt H, Beck C, Unal O, Emmrich P, Arndt H J, *et al*. Characterization of potassium channels in respiratory cells. I. General properties. *Pflugers Arch* 1989; **414:** 291-6.

20 Kunzelmann K, Pavenstadt H, Greger R. Characterization of potassium channels in respiratory cells. II. Inhibitors and regulation. *Pflugers Arch* 1989; **414:** 297-303.

21 Henderson RM, Brayden DJ, Roberts M, Cuthbert AW. Potassium channels in primary cultures of human eccrine sweat gland cells. *J Physiol* 1990; **425:** 68.

22 Henderson RM, Cuthbert AW. A high conductance $Ca^{2}+$ -activated K+ channel in cultured human eccrine sweat gland cells. *Pflugers Arch* 1991; **418:** 271-275.

23 Henderson RM, Cuthbert AW. An outward-rectifying potassium channel in cultured cystic fibrosis human eccrine sweat-gland cells. *J Physiol* 1991; **434:** 92.

24 Gregory RJ, Cheng SH, Rich DP, Marshall J, Paul S, Hehir K, *et al.* Expression and characterization of the cystic fibrosis transmembrane conductance regulator. *Nature* 1990; **347:** 382-6.

25 Rich DP, Anderson MP, Gregory RJ, Cheng SH, Paul S, Jefferson DM, *et al.* Expression of cystic fibrosis transmembrane conductance regulator corrects defective chloride channel regulation in cystic fibrosis airway epithelial cells. *Nature* 1990; **347:** 358-63.

26 Cheng PW, Boat TF, Cranfill K, Yankaskas JR, Boucher RC. Increased sulfation of glycoconjugates by cultured nasal epithelial cells from patients with cystic fibrosis. *J Clin Invest* 1989; **84:** 68-72.

27 Ford JM, Hait WN. Pharmacology of drugs that alter multidrug resistance in cancer. *Pharmacol Rev* 1990; **42:** 155-99.

28 Cheng SH, Gregory RJ, Marshall J, Paul S, Souza DW, White GA, *et al.* Defective intracellular transport and processing of CFTR is the molecular basis of most cystic fibrosis. *Cell* 1990; **63:** 827-34.

29 Anderson MP, Rich DP, Gregory RJ, Smith AE, Welsh MJ. Generation of cAMP-activated chloride currents by expression of CFTR. *Science* 1991; **251:** 679-82.

30 Cuthbert AW, *et al.* In: *Amiloride and Epithelial Sodium Transport.* Urban & Schwarzanberg, Munich, 1979.

31 Knowles MR, Church NL, Waltner WE, Yankaskas JR, Gilligan P, King M, *et al.* A study of aerosolised amiloride for the treatment of lung disease in cystic fibrosis. *New Engl J Med* 1990; **322:** 1189-94.

DISCUSSION

Dr David What actually happens to the transport and secretion of chloride in the stomach in cystic fibrosis, and how might that be affected if you were able to stimulate chloride transport?

Professor Cuthbert In relation to gastric acid secretion very little as far as I know. The mechanisms are quite different and I have no information on altered gastric secretion in CF. The lung is a particularly easy organ to get at. I could imagine that a nebulised drug would get at the chloride channels in the apical membranes of the airway epithelium and that drug could be cleared from the body without ever seeing gastric mucosa. I think the chloride channels of the gastric mucosa are very different from those of the airway.

Dr Nelson You are the first speaker I have heard say that CFTR is a chloride channel. The evidence has been that it is not, but is a member of a large family of membrane related functions, all of which involve outward functioning channels. In CF, the sweat duct in particular is an inward functioning chloride channel which is not working. In the different tissues of the body the chloride channels which are affected in cystic fibrosis are not necessarily the same structures.

Professor Cuthbert If you had heard me speak about a month and half ago I would have said the same, but this field is moving so rapidly that if you put the CFTR DNA into HeLa cells you cause the appearance of new chloride conductors in cells which are not epithelial and nothing to do with CF. That constrains you to believe it is much more likely that it is chloride channels. If we could make CFTR, which nobody can do yet, and incorporate it into a lipid bilayer so that it is an artificially tested and made protein, and it then has a chloride conductance, it has to be a chloride channel. On the other hand it could be very much more subtle. In the HeLa cell CFTR could be used inside something like an NDR protein that is kicking out something nasty from the cells, exposing nascent chloride channels in HeLa cells which do not function because they have got no NDR. With regard to the different sorts of chloride channel I can think of at least five, and there may be others that have such a small conductance and are open for such a short fraction of time that they cannot be detected.

Audience Can you identify the differences in the behaviour of the chloride channels between patients with different types of mutations?

Professor Cuthbert No. I think soon it will no longer be satisfactory to publish biophysics papers about CF tissues unless information on the genetics of those patients is also available. I read a paper recently about unusual potassium flux which was recorded in tissues grown from CF patients, but only four out of five patients gave this result, the other one gave a different result which was also not normal. Perhaps that odd patient had one of the 70 or so non Δ 508 mutations and was homozygous for such. The "structure activity relationships" of the CFTR are going to give us an enormous number of clues about what it is actually doing.

THE GUT IN CYSTIC FIBROSIS IN CHILDHOOD

R. Nelson
Department of Paediatrics,
Royal Victoria Infirmary, Newcastle Upon Tyne

INTRODUCTION

A strong feature of cystic fibrosis is the large number of complications that can affect patients with the disease. They can affect many organ systems, but none can compare with the gastrointestinal tract for the number and the diversity of potential problems and complications. All regions from the oesophagus to the rectum, including the liver and biliary system, may be involved. Over forty complications have been described. These include several disorders which are usually rare in children and young adults such as duodenal ulcer, non-pigment gallstones with cholecystitis, biliary cirrhosis and acute pancreatitis. There are also several seemingly unconnected diseases which appear to occur more commonly in cystic fibrosis than would be expected by chance. These include coeliac disease, cow's milk protein intolerance and enteropathy, Crohn's disease, giardiasis and certain rare carcinomas of the gastrointestinal tract.

GASTROINTESTINAL DISEASES POSSIBLY ASSOCIATED WITH CYSTIC FIBROSIS

Coeliac Disease

Several anecdotal cases of the coexistence of cystic fibrosis and coeliac disease have been reported. An incidence of 1 : 220 was described in a population of 1100 CF patients. This is greater than the highest incidence reported in a normal population.

Cow's Milk Protein Intolerance with Enteropathy

Eight children with cystic fibrosis under the age of three who had abnormal small bowel histology have been reported. They presented with diarrhoea and failure to thrive despite adequate treatment of the pancreatic steatorrhoea. Seven showed an improvement in diarrhoea and an increase in weight gain on a diet free of cow's milk protein.

Giardiasis

Cystic fibrosis patients were found to have a significantly higher rate of infestation with *Giardia lamblia* (28%) compared with a control group of normal members of the same household (6.3%). Cystic fibrosis appeared to be the only risk factor likely to account for the difference in infestation as discovered by counterimmune electrophoresis of faecal samples.

Crohn's Disease

Coexistence of CF and inflammatory bowel disease has rarely been reported. Three cases of Crohn's disease were diagnosed over five years in a CF clinic of 120 patients. The authors suggested that the coexistence of the two conditions was not coincidental, with a frequency much higher than calculated by chance. Fistula formation seemed to be more common in CF patients.

Intestinal Carcinomas

Since 1982 seven adenocarcinomas of the gastrointestinal tract have been described in young adults with cystic fibrosis. There have been one adenoma of the extra hepatic biliary duct system, three adenocarcinomas of the ileum and three adenocarcinomas of the pancreas. Clearly these carcinomas may be associated with cystic fibrosis by chance but the rarity of such tumours in the normal population and the young age of the patients affected (23-42 years, mean 30 years), suggest that young adults with cystic fibrosis may have an increased risk of certain gastrointestinal malignancies.

MALABSORPTION

The basic defect in cystic fibrosis involves deficient transfer of chloride ions across the apical membrane of surface epithelia. In the pancreas this affects the secretion of bicarbonate ions by the cells lining the collecting ducts. The anion exchange mechanism for this secretion involving bicarbonate and chloride ions is secondarily affected by the defect in chloride secretion. In cystic fibrosis therefore the pancreatic exocrine secretions have a lower bicarbonate, lower pH and lower volume than the secretion of normal individuals. These changes affect the physical properties of proteins and mucus within the lumen, resulting in obstruction to the small ducts and secondary damage to pancreatic digestive enzyme secretion. In over 90% of patients seen in the UK with cystic fibrosis the damage to digestive enzyme output by the acini is sufficient to cause malabsorption.

In many patients the malabsorption of cystic fibrosis is not solely related to the pancreatic exocrine damage. Other gastrointestinal problems such as gastric hypersecretion, reduced duodenal bicarbonate concentration and pH, disorders of bile acid metabolism and altered intestinal motility and permeability may all contribute to malabsorption or affect its response to treatment.

Treatment of Pancreatic Malabsorption

The basis for treatment of pancreatic exocrine failure is administration of pancreatic supplements with each meal. In modern preparations the active enzymes are packaged in microspheres surrounded by a pH sensitive hydrocarbon membrane which protects the enzymes from destruction by gastric acidity within the stomach. At a pH of 5.5 to 6.0 the microspheres dissolve, releasing the active enzymes into the duodenal lumen. Currently there are three preparations in use in the United

Kingdom: Pancrease, Creon and Nutrizyme GR. There are differences between the three preparations in the quantity of enzymes obtained within each capsule and differences in the efficient release of enzymes at duodenal pH levels. Despite this, clinically there appears to be very little difference in their ability to control pancreatic steatorrhoea.

In the majority of patients pancreatic enzyme supplements partially correct malabsorption sufficient to support satisfactory growth and weight gain. A small proportion however continue to have severe steatorrhoea despite large numbers of enzyme capsules daily. Further increases in enzyme supplements are unlikely to further improve malabsorption, which is probably related to other gastrointestinal factors. In one study of patients receiving large doses the number of capsules was reduced without significantly affecting fat excretion.

Effects of Reduced Duodenal pH on Malabsorption and its Treatment

The acid pH within the duodenal lumen in cystic fibrosis may affect the response to enzyme supplementation by reducing the release of enzymes from the microspheres because the pH may remain below 5. Below this pH the pancreatic enzymes lipase, trypsin and amylase will also be progressively inactivated on release from the microspheres. Studies of fasting ambulatory recordings of pH throughout the upper small intestine suggest that although duodenal pH is more acid than normal controls there are usually sufficient periods when the pH is above 6 to allow normal release and activity of supplementary enzymes in the upper small intestine.

Patients with persistent malabsorption despite large doses of enzyme supplementation therefore are likely to have other factors responsible for their persistent malabsorption. At a low duodenal pH bile acids, particularly glycine conjugated, are precipitated and inactivated. When fatty acid concentrations exceed the solubilising ability of bile acids, they are partitioned between an emulsified oil phase and a mixed micellar phase. The distribution of fatty acids between the two phases is highly dependent upon luminal pH and on the chain length of the fatty acid. Below pH 6.0 the partition of long chain fatty acids increasingly favours the emulsified oil phase.

Disorders of Bile Acid Metabolism

Cystic fibrosis is characterised by multiple alterations in bile acid metabolism. The cells lining the bile canaliculi of the liver have a similar disorder of ion secretion to the pancreatic collecting duct epithelium. There is therefore a reduced concentration of bicarbonate in hepatic bile, lowering the pH. This is associated with a decreased bile volume and bile acid independent bile flow. pH mediated changes in mucus and protein within the bile canaliculi are partly responsible for the cholestasis characterised by increased fasting and post prandial serum bile acid concentrations. These changes may be responsible for the development of biliary cirrhosis characteristic of cystic fibrosis.

The other major change in bile acid metabolism is increased faecal excretion. In normal individuals less than 3% of the total bile acid pool is excreted in the faeces daily as there is a very efficient enterohepatic circulation of bile acids, mainly the result of ileal absorption from the intestinal lumen into the portal venous system. It is estimated that during the digestion and absorption of a single meal the bile acid pool will circulate fully 2-3 times. A large proportion of the increased faecal excretion of bile acids in cystic fibrosis is related to malabsorption whereby bile acids are bound to unabsorbed food residue entering the colon. There is also some evidence that there may be an inherent ileal malabsorption in cystic fibrosis.

The result of these changes in bile acid metabolism is a reduced bile acid pool. Studies of duodenal bile acid output during a test meal show variable bile acid concentrations. Total bile acid output is reduced with delayed appearance and peak concentrations of bile acids following the stimulation of a test meal compared with normal controls. Because of the low bile volume many patients have normal or high bile acid concentrations. Only occasional patients have duodenal bile acid concentrations below the critical micellar concentration.

In cholestasis there is characteristically a reduction in the ratio of glycine conjugated bile acids to taurine conjugated bile acids (the glycine taurine ratio). Increased faecal excretion would tend to increase the glycine taurine ratio. In cystic fibrosis the glycine taurine ratio is characteristically increased. This increases the problem of bile acid precipitation at acid duodenal pH because glycine conjugates are much more susceptible to this process. Evidence therefore suggests that patients with cystic fibrosis have a functional taurine deficiency and studies have demonstrated improved fat absorption on taurine supplements.

Some patients show evidence of bile acid deconjugation as demonstrated by the C^{14} glycocholate breath test (see later).

Other Gastrointestinal Changes which Affect Malabsorption and the Response to its Treatment

Delayed intestinal transit is another change in gastrointestinal function described in cystic fibrosis. This may be an inherent feature of cystic fibrosis, or may be mediated via the malabsorption by the establishment of the 'ileal brake'. This phenomenon has been demonstrated where the instillation of partially digested lipid into the ileum causes hormonal slowing of small intestinal transit. This may contribute to partial obstruction of the distal small intestine. Both of these problems are occasionally associated with small bowel bacterial contamination and bile acid deconjugation in cystic fibrosis. Single cases have been reported where the administration of cisapride to increase small intestinal motility has been associated with a marked improvement in malabsorption and weight gain. In the majority of studies involving larger numbers of patients however, cisapride has not been associated with any significant improvement in malabsorption.

Choice of Treatment for Resistant Malabsorption

Some patients with cystic fibrosis continue to have severe malabsorption despite high doses of pancreatic supplements. Increasing the pancreatic supplements is often not associated with any improvement in fat absorption and one study has shown no change in faecal fat excretion when high dose pancreatic supplements were halved. Sometimes an improvement in the malabsorption may result from a change from one commercially available pancreatic supplement to another.

Several studies have shown little significant change in fat absorption when H_2 antagonists, such as cimetidine or ranitidine, are added to pancreatic microspheres. Other suppressors of gastric acid secretion such as prostaglandin E_1 analogues and particularly the proton pump inhibitor, omeprazole may be more effective. Omeprazole is a much more powerful suppressor of gastric acid output, producing significant changes in gastric pH, and is more effective in suppressing post prandial gastric acid secretion. There has been considerable discussion in the medical literature about the risk of gastric tumours following the prolonged use of all of these drugs. They should therefore be used with caution for prolonged medication in cystic fibrosis only where nutrition is severely compromised and where other potentially safer treatments have failed. Patients with cystic fibrosis may already have an inherent increased risk of gastrointestinal tumours.

Bile acid supplementation with ursodeoxycholic acid has been used in cystic fibrosis, particularly for the treatment and prophylaxis of non-pigment gallstones and also in patients with abnormal liver function tests where its use may reduce the future risk of biliary cirrhosis. In a small number of patients studied, faecal fat excretion was slightly improved on treatment with ursodeoxycholic acid. The detergent properties of ursodeoxycholic acid are less than endogenous primary bile acids but its effect upon ileal absorption of endogenous bile acids may produce changes in the profile of the bile acid pool which result in improved fat solubilisation. Taurine supplementation has also been shown to improve faecal fat excretion in cystic fibrosis. Treatment with ursodeoxycholic acid will further increase the glycine : taurine ratio and therefore taurine supplements are particularly indicated in patients treated with ursodeoxycholic acid.

DISTAL INTESTINAL OBSTRUCTION SYNDROME

This is one of the more common intestinal complications of cystic fibrosis. The incidence varies from centre to centre, but some surveys have reported up to 15% of patients being affected. It only affects patients with pancreatic insufficiency who require enzyme replacement therapy to control malabsorption. The condition tends to occur more commonly in adolescence and adulthood.

The aetiology of the condition is unknown. There is an accumulation of viscid muco-faeculent material and probably calcium soaps in the terminal ileum and caecum. It may be related to a primary defect in clearance of mucus through the intestinal lumen. Pancreatic hyposecretion, protein hyperconcentration and intestinal hyperacidity may contribute to its development. It may also be related to poorly controlled fat malabsorption affecting intestinal transit via the ileal brake mechanism.

Clinically the patients present with a chronic partial intestinal obstruction. Patients experience recurrent episodes of colicky abdominal pain, often exacerbated by the intake of food. The diagnosis is supported by the detection of a palpable faecal mass in the right iliac fossa. Untreated, the condition may contribute to anorexia and weight loss. Radiological studies and abdominal ultrasound may be needed to exclude other conditions such as intussusception, colonic faecal retention and diseases of the appendix.

The mainstays of treatment are various remedies to disturb and flush out the accumulated intestinal contents. Oral N-acetylcysteine has probably been superseded by more effective treatments such as oral sodium diatrizoate (Gastrograffin) or oral balanced intestinal lavage solution (Golytely). Medical treatment is usually effective in reducing the obstruction and controlling symptoms. Intestinal surgery is rarely required.

Prophylactic treatment may include laxatives and increased dietary roughage. Attempts should be made to improve fat absorption by increasing enzyme supplements, increasing gastric and duodenal pH and possibly supplementing calorie intake with medium chain triglycerides. Two unreported controlled trials of cisapride showed no difference in the rate of recurrence on cisapride or on placebo.

We have experienced three patients with severe, almost total, intestinal obstruction. In one of these patients the development of intestinal obstruction was probably related to the administration of nebulised ipratropium. All three patients experienced persistent intestinal obstruction demonstrated radiologically following the administration of oral Gastrograffin. The administration of cisapride by suppository was followed by the resumption of defaecation, rapid movement of radiopaque material from the ileum into the colon and rectum and resolution of the obstruction.

SUMMARY

Many conditions other than exocrine pancreatic hyposecretion affect the gastrointestinal tract in cystic fibrosis more frequently than in the general population. Some, eg. distal intestinal obstruction, are unique complications of cystic fibrosis. Complex intestinal problems may contribute to severe malabsorption in selected patients.

REFERENCES

Zentler-Munro PL. Cystic Fibrosis a gastrointestinal cornucopia. *Gut* 1987; **28:** 1531-1547

Park RW, Grand RJ. Gastrointestinal manifestations of cystic fibrosis - A Review. *Gastroenterology* 1981; **81:** 1143-61.

Velletta EA, Mestelle G. Incidence of coeliac disease in a cystic fibrosis population. *Acta Paediatr Scand* 1989; **78:** 784-785.

Behrens R, Segerer H, Bowing B, Bender SW. Crohns disease in cystic fibrosis. *J Pediatr Gastroenterol Nutr* 1989; **9:** 528-531.

Stead RJ, Pedington AN, Hinks LJ, Clayton BE, Hodson ME, Betten JC. Selenium deficiency and possible increased risk of carcinoma in adults with cystic fibrosis. *Lancet* 1985; **ii:** 862-863.

Littlewood JM, Kelleher J, Walters MP, Johnson AW, Pediatr J. *In vivo* and *in vitro* studies of microsphere pancreatic supplements. *Gastroenterol Nutr* 1988; **7**(suppl. 1)**:** s22-s29.

Gow R, Bradbear R, Francis P, Shepherd R. Comparative study of varying regimes to improve steatorrhoea and creatorrhoea in cystic fibrosis: effectiveness of an enteric coated preperation with and without antacids and cimetidine. *Lancet* 1981; **ii:** 1071-1074.

Robb TA, Davidson GP, Kirubakaran C. Conjugated bile acids in serum and secretions in response to cholecystolin/secretion stimulation in children with cystic fibrosis. *Gut* 1985; **26:** 1246-1256.

Harries JT, Muller DPR, McCollum JPK, Lipson A, Roma E, Norman AP. Intestinal bile acids in cystic fibrosis. *Arch Dis Child* 1979; **54:** 19-24.

Goodchild MC, Murphy GM, Howell AM, Natler SA, Anderson CM. Aspects of bile acid metabolism in cystic fibrosis. *Arch Dis Child* 1975; **50:** 769-778.

Reduced intraluminal bile acid concentrations and fat maldigestion in pancreatic insufficiency: correction by treatment. *Gastroenterology* 1979; **77:** 285-289.

Weizman Z, Durie PR, Kopelman HR, Vesely SM, Forstner GG. Bile acid secretion in cystic fibrosis: evidence of a defect unrelated to fat malabsorption. *Gut* 1986; **27:** 1043-1048.

Zentler-Munro PL, Fitzpatrick WJF, Batten JC, Northfield TC. Effect of intra jejunal acidity on aqueous phase bile acid and lipid concentrations in pancreatic steatorrhoea due to cystic fibrosis. *Gut* 1984; **25:** 500-507.

Santamaria F, Oggero V, Raia V, Salvatori D, Vittoria L, de Ritis G. Cisapride and cystic fibrosis. *Pediatr J Gastroenterol Nutr* 1989; **9:** 539-542.

O'Halloran SM, Gilbert J, McKendrick OM, Carty HML, Heef DP. Gastrograffin in acute meconium ileus equivalent. *Arch Dis Child* 1986; **61:** 1128-30.

Gleghorn GJ, Stringer DA, Forstner GG, Durie PR. Treatment of distal intestinal obstruction syndrome in cystic fibrosis with a balanced intestinal lavage solution. *Lancet* 1986; **i:** 8-11.

Bali A, Stebleforth DE, Asquith P. Prolonged small intestinal transit time in cystic fibrosis. *Br Med J* 1983; **287:** 1011-1013.

Darling PB, Lepage G, Leroy C, Masson P, Roy CC. Effect of taurine supplements on fat absorption in cystic fibrosis. *Paediatr Res* 1985; **19:** 578-582.

DISCUSSION

Dr David Would you recommend that a patient with cystic fibrosis should be looked after by a gastroenterologist or a respiratory physician?

Dr Nelson Most adult patients should be treated by chest physicians because the main problems are in the chest. However they have so many potential GI problems that there should be some gastroentestinal input.

Audience You mentioned using cisapride to improve motility in distal small bowel obstruction. Has anybody used erythromycin?

Dr Nelson As far as I know not. I do not think erythromycin would work as well since as I understand it, its main effect is on gastric emptying whereas cisapride produces co-ordinated motor activity throughout the GI tract. I would like to enlarge on the use of the H2 antagonists, the prostoglandin analogue misoprostol and omeprazole, for the treatment of gastric acidity. At the present time there is much discussion about the long term safety of these drugs and the fact that they may be associated with tumours. The argument is that they are relatively safe but even cimetidine has only been on the market for 13 years, and there is very little information beyond 6 years continuous treatment. There is a role for these drugs, but they have to be used carefully, for patients where there is a severe problem, and not routinely; especially since there may already be an increased risk of cancer in the CF patients.

Audience Did you measure gastric levels?

Dr Nelson That is important in relationship to omeprazole, where there is a potential risk. Animal studies show that rats in particular developed carcinoid tumours in the stomach, and this was related to the very high gastric levels of omeprazole that some of these animals achieved as a result of the marked depression of gastric acidity. We would certainly measure gastric levels regularly on these patients.

Audience Would you like to comment on the role of ursodeoxycholic acid in the young population?

Dr Nelson Ursodeoxycholic acid and taurine supplements may improve fat absorption. Of the two, taurine supplements are likely to be more effective. Ursodeoxycholic acid has been used to treat patients with gallstones or patients where there is a risk of their actually developing liver disease in particular. In patients that have liver disease it gives a small improvement in fat absorption but the numbers are small. It is important that if ursodeoxycholic acid is given to these patients taurine is also given, because ursodeoxycholic acid increases the faecal excretion of endogenous bile acids (as a result of a competition for ileal absorption between ursodeoxycholic acid and the endogenous bile acids). You are actually likely to get an even further increase in GT ratio in these liver patients.

NUTRITION IN CYSTIC FIBROSIS

C J Taylor
Department of Paediatrics, University of Sheffield

INTRODUCTION

Cystic Fibrosis (CF) is currently perceived as a chest disease with intestinal complications, yet historically the disease was seen as an intestinal disorder with respiratory complications! This interpretation is not difficult to follow when, as recently as the 1950s, many CF children were dying in early infancy from malnutrition, often before recurrent respiratory infections became evident. Even in recent years many physicians caring for patients with CF considered growth failure to be an inevitable consequence of the disease. However, by the mid 1970s the importance of nutrition began to be appreciated. Unambiguous links between weight gain and survival emerged[1]. It became clear that patients with "normal" fat absorption showed an improved respiratory prognosis[2] and that protein calorie malnutrition carried a particularly ominous prognosis[3]. Yet it is only since pioneering work of clinics such as Toronto in the 1970s, where an aggressive nutritional policy was followed[4], that it has been realised that near normal growth could be achieved.

In 1962 Sproul and Huang[5] reported growth patterns for a group of 50 CF patients. Between 0 and 2 years both sexes showed growth velocities between the third and tenth centiles; weight gain decreased progressively, falling below the third centile at 11 years and continued to fall away till 16 years. Linear growth was maintained between the third and tenth centiles till 12 years then plateaued during early adolescence in both sexes. A further report in 1975[6] continued to demonstrate a relentless decline in weight below the third centile by 15 years of age. The Toronto experience[7] now shows that mean heights for males and females between the 42nd and 44th centiles can be expected throughout childhood and adolescence. The weights for male patients show the same pattern, but mean weights for females lie about the 31st centile. This improvement in nutrition can now be seen as a survival advantage.

Causes of malnutrition:
Poor nutrition in CF results from 3 factors that are often interlinked:
1.   Degree of malabsorption.
2.   Increased energy demands of the disease.
3.   Dietary intake.

1. Malabsorption

Over 85% of CF patients have overt steatorrhoea; even those with a degree of pancreatic sufficiency show defective production of water and bicarbonate in pancreatic secretions. This anomaly alone disturbs the digestive milieu of the upper intestine, as the failure to neutralise gastric contents leads to bile salt inactivation, and the abnormal protonation of fatty acids by luminal acid inhibits micellar dispersion (Figure 1)[8]. The administration of exogenous pancreatic enzymes rarely abolishes steatorrhoea. Pancreatic lipase is rapidly and irreversibly inactivated at pH<4, thus as little as 22% of the trypsin and 8% of the lipase of conventional pancreatic enzyme preparations are delivered to the intestine[9]. However, porcine pancreatic enzymes encapsulated in acid resistant enteric coated microspheres can maximise delivery of active enzyme to the small bowel[10]. Endogenous lipase is also protected from degradation by a protease inhibitor during duodenal-ileal transit; in its absence lipase becomes sensitive to proteolytic activity and particularly to chymotrypsin. The addition of exogenous chymotrypsin can even increase the degradation of lipase, exacerbating steatorrhoea[11]. Thus it has been suggested that the lipase content of microsphere preparations should be increased to allow a minimal chymotrypsin/lipase ratio[12].

Many unsuccessful attempts have been made to enhance enzyme function by inhibiting [13,14] or neutralising gastric acid[15], or by enhancing bile salt function with synthetic detergent[16]. N-acetyl cysteine has also been used to reduce the mucus layer overlying the intestinal epithelium in the belief that it may act as a barrier to absorption - with uncovincing results.

- Lipase, trypsin and amylase progressively inactivated at pH<5.

- Excess faecal bile acid loss

- Enhanced hepatic synthesis of bile acids with glycine taurine ratio in excess of 6:1 *(normal 2:1)*

- Glycine conjugated bile salts precipitate at pH<5 *(50% compared with trace amounts of taurine conjugates)*

- Failure of protonation of fatty acids, necessary for transport across microvillus membrane. *(protonation occurs in the acidic bulk phase, impairing micellar dispersion)*.

Figure 1. The effects of the acidic CF jejunum on absorption.

2. Increased energy demands of the disease

The basal metabolic rate (BMR) correlates with body size and in sedentary adults accounts for three-quarters of daily energy expenditure. In CF, where a combination of obstructive and restrictive changes increase the work of breathing, a 30% increase in BMR has been reported[17]. This figure approximates to results of more extensive studies in adults with chronic bronchitis and emphysema, where the resting energy expenditure is increased to 140% of predicted[18]. Total energy expenditure is also 25% higher in CF infants without chronic lung disease than in normals, implicating either the caloric demands of subclinical lung disease or the possibility of an energy-requiring basic defect[19]. If this increased energy requirement is not met, growth failure will result.

The adaptive response to malnutrition in CF is also abnormal. In the normal child, even with a degree of protein-calorie malnutrition, the response to infection is an increase in protein synthesis. CF children, however, exhibit a marked decrease in protein synthesis with acute pulmonary infection. Stable but chronically infected CF patients have also been shown to be in a state of protein catabolism, and will therefore tolerate acute infections poorly[20]. In malnourished CF children stunting may also be seen despite a maintained calorie intake, reflecting the increased work of breathing associated with unrecognised respiratory infection.

3. Deficient intake

Deficient intake appears to be the chief reason for growth failure in CF[21]. The contribution of low fat diets to poor nutrition has long been recognised[22] yet many children still consume only 80% of the recommended daily allowances for energy and protein[23]. Dietary comparisons of patients from a single clinic have clearly demonstrated an association between malnourishment and low fat diets. Well nourished patients were found to take a significantly higher fat (116.4g/day) and energy intake (116% RDA) than malnourished patients who received 90% RDA for energy intake and had continued to take a low fat diet (89.9g/day)[24]. During pulmonary exacerbations energy requirements increase to meet the immune response to infection, yet the appetite usually diminishes. An inadequate intake means that "catch up" is often inadequate leading to a familiar pattern of slow weight loss punctuated by acute step-like episodes of weight loss associated with further chest infections (Figure 2).

Vitamins and Trace Elements

Micronutrient status can also influence both growth and immune competence. As trace metal absorption proceeds most efficiently in the proximal small bowel and is mediated by specific binding ligands present in pancreatic secretions and or mucosal cells[25], CF children with pancreatic exocrine deficiency and impaired absorption are at risk of secondary deficiency of these essential micronutrients.

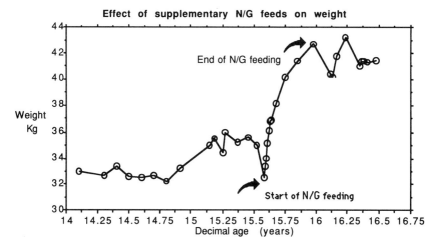

Figure 2. Demonstration of enhanced weight gain with supplementary naso-gastric feeding using a Silk & Corsafe enteral feeding tube *(E Merck Ltd)* and a milk-based overnight feed (Fortison Energy Plus: 5% caseinates, 17.9% maltodextrin, 6.5% fat: 0.63 MJ/100ml; *(Cow & Gate)*.

Zinc is an essential nutrient in man and low serum levels have been described in CF children[26]. Nutritional dwarfism and retarded pubertal development are both associated with zinc deficiency, and can be reversed by zinc supplementation[27]. Zinc deficiency in experimental animals leads to thymic atrophy, and associated defects in cell mediated immunity and T-helper cell function. Abnormalities in both pancreatic and intestinal epithelium have also been described, as have detectable differences in taste acuity[28]. Studies of short term zinc supplementation in CF patients have been disappointing and only anecdotal reports of improved growth and pubertal development following zinc supplementation exist[29].

Iron absorption appears normal in treated CF children[30], however biochemical selenium deficiency has been described[31,32]. Others have reported both serum concentrations and red cell glutathione peroxidase activity are usually normal[33]. While treatable deficiencies should be avoided, blind supplementation with trace element mixtures is undesirable as toxicity is easily induced[34] and accumulations, particularly of copper can develop, leading in turn to the risk of secondary liver damage and the development of cirrhosis, one of the late manifestations of CF[35].

It is common practice to supplement CF patients with fat soluble vitamins. Vitamin A levels may be low in 40% of CF patients even with conventional supplements [36]. Whether this represents a true deficiency is debatable as liver stores are frequently high and serum levels may show little response to oral

30

supplements. This suggests that it may be the transport in plasma that is defective, and plasma retinol binding protein levels are often below normal[37]. Recently Rayner *et al* have demonstrated night blindness and conjuctival xerosis in CF adolescents, which have responded to large doses (1-200,000 IU) of water miscible vitamin A [38]. Serum 25-OH cholecalciferol levels can also be reduced but clinical rickets does not occur in the absence of associated liver or renal tubular disease[39,40] and vitamin K deficiency is rare[41]. Vitamin E levels are nearly always low unless supplements are given[42] and deficiency states have been reported[43]. It is not clear whether CF patients require additional water soluble vitamins. B_1, B_2 and B_6 status together with folic acid level appear satisfactory, however vitamin C and B_{12}[44] may be deficient in individual patients. Deficiency states are also associated with defective immune competence (see Table 1).

Can Nutrition be improved?
The encouragement of a normal high calorie, high protein diet (120-150% RDA) will, in the absence of significant pulmonary disease, produce adequate growth in the majority of CF children even with a modest residual steatorrhoea. In other cases an improvement in nutrition can be achieved by simple means including the use of pre-mixed and powdered dietary supplements (See appendix) and the prescription of sufficient enteric coated microsphere pancreatic enzymes to control malabsorption. In more severely malnourished patients anorexia is often a problem and oral supplements of varying palatability are frequently rejected. Under these circumstances some form of invasive nutritional intervention is necessary (Figure 2).

Studies using both enteral and intravenous routes have been reported, with nasogastric tubes and gastrostomy or jejunostomy tubes being used as enteral delivery systems. Significant weight gains have been achieved using supplementary parenteral nutrition in both the short and long term. Two studies have also demonstrated an improvement in pulmonary function[45,46]. Long-term supplementation via both gastrostomy (mean 1.1 years)[47] and jejunostomy (10-36 months)[48]

TABLE 1. Effects of vitamin deficiencies on immunity

Deficiency	Humoral	Cell mediated
Vitamin A	⇩	⇩
Vitamin B	⇩	⇩
Vitamin B_2	⇩	⇩
Vitamin B_6	⇩	⇩
Vitamin B_{12}	⇩	⇩
Vitamin C		⇩
Folic acid	⇩	⇩

also produced either an acceleration in growth velocity or improved weight for height. In neither study did the expected decline in pulmonary function occur. Complications in both studies were said to be mild. Endoscopic placement of percutaneous gastrostomy tubes under local anaesthesia makes the former technique particularly attractive[49]. Refeeding produces a demonstrable increase in both body fat and lean body mass, however, the resting energy expenditure also increases, increasing the subsequent caloric needs of CF patients[50]. Treatment may also be a factor in increasing energy demands by as much as 10%, as Vaisman et al demonstrated by studying the effects of salbutamol, a ß agonist, on heart rate and resting energy expenditure[51].

APPENDIX

Selection of enteral feeding supplements

* **Fortisip** - 200ml cartons containing 5% caseinates, 17.9% low - lactose carbohydrate, 6.5% fat: 0.63MJ/100ml; *(Cow & Gate)*

  Fresubin - 200ml carton with straw containing 3.8% milk and soy protein, 13.8% maize starch, 3.4% sunflower oil: 0.42MJ/100ml; *(Fresenius)*

  Fortison - 4% caseinates, 12.1% maltodextrin, 3.9% fat: 0.42MJ/100ml; *(Cow & Gate)*

  Fortison Energy Plus - protein 6%, carbohydrate 18.3%, fat 5.8%: 0.64MJ/100ml; *(Cow & Gate)*

  Ensure - 237ml bottles and 250ml cans containing 3.7% milk and soy protein, 14.6% corn syrup and sucrose, 3.7% corn oil: 0.45MJ/100ml; *(Abbott)*

† **Calogen** - Arachis oil 50% in water: 1.88MJ/100ml; *(SHS)*

  Maxijul - powder, powder glucose polymer: 1.5MJ/100g; *(SHS)* also liquid (200ml, 0.8MJ/100ml)

  Polycal - maltodextrin syrup: *(Cow & Gate)*

  Caloreen - glucose polymer: power, 1.67MJ/100g; *(Roussel)* also liquid (250g)

  (*Pre-prepared liquid feeds; †Powders and emulsions suitable for adding to drinks)

REFERENCES

1 Kraemer R, Rudeberg A, Hadorn B, Rossi E. Relative underweight in cystic fibrosis and its prognostic value. *Acta Paediatr Scand* 1978; **67:** 33-7.

2 Gaskin K, Gurwitz D, Durie P, Corey M, Levison H, Forstner G. Improved respiratory prognosis in patients with cystic fibrosis with normal fat absorption. *J Pediatr* 1982; **100:** 857-62.

3 Abman SH, Accurso FJ, Bowman CM. Persistent morbidity and mortality of protein-calorie malnutrition in young infants with cystic fibrosis. *J Pediatr Gastroenterol Nutr* 1986; **5:** 393-96.

4   Crozier DN. Cystic fibrosis - a not so fatal disease. *Pediatr Clin North Am* 1974; **21:** 935-50.

5   Sproul A, Huang H. Growth patterns in children with cystic fibrosis. *J Pediatr* 1964; **65:** 664-76.

6   Berry HK, Kellogg FW, Hunt MM, Ingberg RL, Richter L, Gutjahr C. Dietary supplement and nutrition in children with cystic fibrosis. *Am J Dis Child* 1975; **129:** 165-71.

7   Corey M, McLaughlin FJ, Williams M, Levison H. A Comparison of survival, growth, and pulmonary function in patients with cystic fibrosis in Boston and Toronto. *J Clin Epidemiol* 1988; **41:** 583-91.

8   Regan PT, Malagelada JR, Di Magno EP, Go VLW. Reduced intraluminal bile acid concentrations and fat maldigestion in pancreatic insufficiency: correction by treatment. *Gastroenterology* 1979; **77:** 285-89.

9   DiMagno EP, Malagelada JR, Go VLW, Moertel CG. Fate of orally ingested enzymes in pancreatic insufficiency: Comparison of two dosage schedules. *N Engl J Med* 1977; **296:** 1318-22.

10 Littlewood JM, Kelleher J, Walters MP, Johnson AW. *In vivo* and *in vitro* studies of microsphere pancreatic supplements. *J Pediatr Gastroenterol Nutr* 1988; **7**(suppl 1)**:** S22-9.

11 George DE, Mangos JA. Nutritional management and pancreatic enzyme therapy in cystic fibrosis patients: State of the art in 1987 and projections into the future. *J Pediatr Gastroenterol Nutr* 1988: **7**(suppl 1)**:** S49-57.

12 DiMagno EP. Controversies in the treatment of exocrine pancreatic insufficiency. *Dig Dis Sci* 1982; **27:** 481-84.

13 Cox KL. Isenberg JW, Asher AB, Dooley RR. The effect of cimetidine on maldigestion in cystic fibrosis. *J Pediatr* 1979; **94:** 488-92.

14 De Bieville F, Neijens HJ, Fernandes J, Van Caillie M, Kerrebijn KF. Cimetidine as an adjunct to oral enzymes in the treatment of malabsorption due to cystic fibrosis. *Acta Paediatr Scand* 1981; **70:** 33-7.

15 Gow R, Francis P, Bradbear R, Shepherd R. Comparative study of varying regimens to improve steatorrhoea and creatorrhoea in cystic fibrosis: Effectiveness of an enteric-coated preparation with and without antacids and cimetidine. *Lancet* 1981; **1:** 1071-74.

16 Bouquet J, Sinaasappel M, Neijens HJ. Malabsorption in cystic fibrosis: mechanisms and treatment. *J Pediatr Gastroenterol Nutr* 1988; **7**(suppl 1)**:** S30-5.

17 Adeniyi-Jones S, Suskind R, Kean B. Growth, energy metabolism and T3 levels in malnutrition in cystic fibrosis. *Cystic Fibrosis Club Abstract* 1979; **20:** 22.

18 Wilson DO, Rogers RM, Hoffman RM. Nutrition and chronic lung disease. *Am Rev Respir Dis* 1985; **132:** 1347-65.

19 Shepherd RW, Vasques-Velasquez L, Prentice A, Holt TL, Coward WA, Lucas A. Increased energy expenditure in young children with cystic fibrosis. *Lancet* 1988; **1:** 1300-03.

20 Holt TL, Ward LC, Francis PJ, Isles A, Cooksley WGE, Shepherd RW. Whole body protein turnover in malnourished cystic fibrosis patients and its relationship to pulmonary disease. *Am J Clin Nutr* 1985; **41:** 1061-66.

21 Parsons HG, Beaudry P, Dumas A, Pencharz PB. Energy needs and growth in children with cystic fibrosis. *J Pediatr Gastroenterol Nutr* 1983; **2:** 44-9.

22 Pencharz PB. Energy intakes and low fat diets in children with cystic fibrosis. *J Pediatr Gastroenterol Nutr* 1983; **2:** 400-01.

23 Chase HP, Long MA, Lavin MH. Cystic fibrosis and malnutrition. *J Pediatr* 1979; **95:** 337-42.

24 Soutter VL, Kristidis P, Gruca MA, Gaskin KJ. Chronic undernutrition/growth retardation in cystic fibrosis. *Clin Gastroenterol* 1986; **15:** 137-55.

25 Evans GW, Johnson PE. Copper and zinc binding ligands in the intestinal mucosa. In: Kirchgessner M (ed). *Trace Element Metabolism in Man and Animal.* Munchen: Technische Universitat 1978; 98-105.

26 Palin D, Underwood BA, Denning CR. The effect of oral zinc supplementation on plasma levels of vitamin A and retinol-binding protein in cystic fibrosis. *Am J Clin Nutr* 1979; **32:** 1253-59.

27 Halsted JA, Smith JC. Plasma zinc in health and disease. *Lancet* 1970; **1:** 322-326.

28 Shaw JCL. Trace elements in the fetus and young infant. *Am J Dis Child* 1979; **133:** 1260-68.

29 Dodge JA, Yassa JG. Zinc deficiency syndrome in a British youth with cystic fibrosis. *Br Med J* 1978; **1:** 411.

30 Heinrich HC, Bender-Gotze CH, Gable EE. Absorption of inorganic iron ($^{59}Fe^{2+}$) in relation to iron stores in pancreatic exocrine insufficiency due to cystic fibrosis. *Klin Wochenschr* 1977; **55:** 587-93.

31 Van Caillie-Bertrand M, De Bieville F, Neijens H, Kerrebijn K, Fernandes J, Degenhart HJ. Trace metals in cystic fibrosis. *Acta Paediatr Scand* 1982; **71:** 203-7.

32 Ward KP, Arthur JR, Russell G, Aggett PJ. Blood selenium content and glutathione peroxidase activity in children with cystic fibrosis, coeliac disease asthma and epilepsy. *Eur J Pediatr* 1984; **142:** 21-24.

33 Lloyd-Still JD, Ganther HE. Selenium and glutathione peroxidase in cystic fibrosis. *Pediatrics* 1980; **65:** 1010-12.

34 Hubbard VS, Barbero G, Chase HP. Selenium and cystic fibrosis. *J Pediatr* 1980; **96:** 421-2.

35 Jains S, Scheuer PJ, Samourian S, McGee JO'D, Sherlock S. A controlled trial of D-penicillamine therapy in primary biliary cirrhosis. *Lancet* 1977; **1:** 831-34.

36 Congden PJ, Bruce G, Rothburn MM, Clarke PCN, Littlewood JM, Kelleher J, Losowsky MS. Vitamin status in treated patients with cystic fibrosis. *Arch Dis Child* 1981; **56**: 708-14.

37 Smith FR, Underwood BA, Denning CR, Varma, Goodman DS. Depressed plasma retinol-binding protein levels in cystic fibrosis. *J Lab Clin Med* 1972; **80**: 423-33.

38 Rayner RJ, Tyrrell JC, Hiller EJ, Marenah C, Neugebauer MA, Vernon SA, Brimlow G. Night blindness and conjunctival xerosis caused by vitamin A deficiency in patients with cystic fibrosis. *Arch Dis Child* 1989; **64**: 1151-56.

39 Oppenheimer EH. Focal necrosis of striated muscle in an infant with cystic fibrosis of the pancreas and evidence of lack of absorption of fat soluble vitamins. *Bull Johns Hopkins Hosp* 1956; **98**: 353-59.

40 Scott J, Elias E, Moult PJA, Barnes S, Wills MR. Rickets in adult cystic fibrosis with myopathy, pancreatic insufficiency and proximal renal tubular dysfunction. *Am J Med* 1977; **63**: 488-92.

41 Torstenson OL, Humphrey GB, Edson JR, Warwick WJ. Cystic fibrosis presenting with severe hemorrhage due to vitamin K malabsorption: A report of three cases. *Pediatrics* 1970; **45**: 857-61.

42 Harries JT, Muller DPR. Absorption of different doses of fat soluble and water miscible preparations of vitamin E in children with cystic fibrosis. *Arch Dis Child* 1971; **46**: 341-344.

43 Elias E, Muller DPR, Scott J. Association of spinocerebellar disorders with cystic fibrosis or chronic childhood cholestasis and very low serum vitamin E. *Lancet* 1981; **2**: 1319-21.

44 Deren JJ, Arora B, Toskes PP, Hansell J, Sibinga MS. Malabsorption of crystalline vitamin B12 in cystic fibrosis. *N Engl J Med* 1973; **288**: 949-950.

45 Shepherd R, Cooksley WGE, Domville-Cook WD. Improved growth and clinical nutritional and respiratory changes in response to nutritional therapy in cystic fibrosis. *J Pediatr* 1980; **97**: 351-57.

46 Mansell AL, Anderson JC, Muttart CR, Ores CN, Loeff DS, Levy JS, Heird WC. Short-term pulmonary effects of total parenteral nutrition in children with cystic fibrosis. *J Pediatr* 1984; **104**: 700-05.

47 Levy LD, Durie PR, Pencharz PB, Corey ML. Effects of long term nutritional rehabilitation on body composition and clinical status in malnourished children and adolescents with cystic fibrosis. *J Pediatr* 1985; **107**: 225-30.

48 Boland M, MacDonald NE, Stoski DS, Soucy P, Patrick J. Chronic jejunostomy feeding with a non-elemental formula in undernourished patients with cystic fibrosis. *Lancet* 1986; **1**: 232-234.

49 Gauderer MWL, Ponsky JL, Izant RJ. Gastrostomy without laparotomy: A percutaneous endoscopic technique. *J Pediatr Surg* 1980; **15**: 872-75.

50 Vaisman N, Pencharz PB. Changes in resting energy expenditure (REE) and body composition (BC) on refeeding malnourished patients with cystic fibrosis. *Pediatric Research* 1987; **21:** A640.

51 Vaisman N, Pencharz P, Levy L, Tan Y, Soldin S, Canny G, Hahn E. The effect of salbutamol on resting energy expenditure (REE) in patients with cystic fibrosis. *Pediatric Research* 1987; **21:** A642.

DISCUSSION

Audience A number of patients with CF have a feeding gastrostomy. Is there any evidence of an increase in gastric acidity after gastrostomy?

Dr Nelson I think there is one paper in the literature suggesting that reflux can be affected adversely. In our experience gastrostomies have been remarkably free of complications. There is some evidence that reflux is increased by gastrostomy because you have altered the angle at which the oesophagus enters the stomach, but you are not actually altering the gastric secretion.

TREATMENT OF CHEST DISEASE IN CHILDHOOD CYSTIC FIBROSIS

P Helms
Department of Paediatrics
The Queen Elizabeth Children's Hospital, London

Lung disease remains the single most important cause of morbidity and death in cystic fibrosis (CF). A major objective of treatment is to maintain respiratory function and slow the rate of progressive lung damage. *In utero* lung development is normal and lung cells are normal at birth. Damage is due to retention of secretions, chronic and acute infections with progressive damage to the airway wall going on to bronchiectasis, lung fibrosis, pulmonary hypertension and ultimately respiratory failure.

Since the disease was first characterised in the 1940s survival has improved steadily with median survival now in the mid/late 20s[1,2]. This is mirrored by falling mortality rates in childhood with approximately 40 children under 16 dying annually in the UK (Figure 1). It is apparent that most mortality and serious morbidity has been exported from the paediatric age group into late adolescence and adult life. This is placing considerable strains on adult chest physicians and the service they provide. These financial and emotional burdens need to be recognised and supported.

Screening and Early Treatment

Could paediatricians do better and improve the respiratory health of those teenagers approaching adulthood? Intuitively, one way of doing this would be to identify infants with the disease before they become symptomatic. This hypothesis is behind the many neonatal screening programmes that have been reported during the 1980s. Wilcken and Chalmers[3] concluded from their study that immune re-active trypsin (IRT) screening was able to reduce mortality in terms of hospital admission days. However as was pointed out in the subsequent correspondence, screened patients included those with mild disease who would not normally present until later childhood or even in adult life, and more severely affected infants would be over-represented in the unscreened group. Furthermore a more detailed and longer term prospective study was unable to demonstrate any significant differences over a 4 year follow up, in terms of height and weight centiles[4]. This of course does not mean that neonatal screening has no significance; it may identify first born infants with the disease before the couple have other at risk children. However it is of interest that even in the unscreened group most children are diagnosed before the age of 2 years[4], an observation which again questions the value of mass screening programmes.

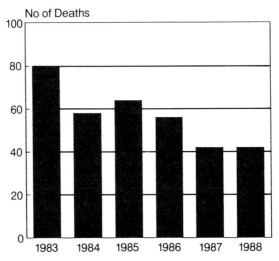

Figure 1. Cystic fibrosis UK child mortality, 1-15 years.

What if persistent focal disease develops? Severe localised bronchiectasis has for many years been dealt with by surgical resection and this procedure has been shown to be safe in CF patients[5]. The need to consider such an approach does not arise very often; for example over the 14 year period 1975-89, in a total CF population of over 350 at Great Ormond Street, only 9 underwent this procedure. Indications were:

1. Severe recurrent symptoms which were difficult to control
2. Failure to thrive
3. Local disease which was beginning to include adjacent areas.

In this series attempts were made to restore normal lung function to the affected area by bronchoscopy and local bronchial lavage without success and the technique is no longer used routinely. The results of resection in carefully selected patients can be dramatic as illustrated in Figure 2. In the hands of an experienced cardiothoracic surgeon, lobectomy is safe and can result in a considerable improvement in quality of life at least in the medium term. Previous thoracic surgery of this type is not a contra-indication to heart-lung transplantation as first thought [6].

Physiotherapy
The aim of physiotherapy is to mobilise and drain as much infected material from the lungs as possible. Although in many asymptomatic infants and very young

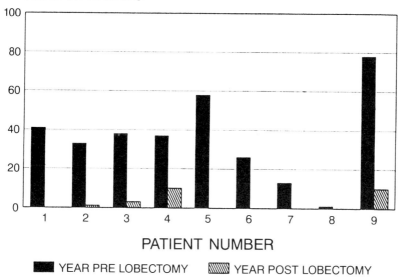

HOSPITAL DAYS

PATIENT NUMBER

■ YEAR PRE LOBECTOMY   ▨ YEAR POST LOBECTOMY

Figure 2. Days spent in hospital in the year before following lobectomy in 9 children with focal disease aged 7 months to 11 years. Five children did not require admission and in the remainder the large reduction in hospital days can be clearly seen.

children this may not produce an obvious result, it is important to establish a regular treatment regime in order to reinforce good habits that will, it is hoped, remain with the child as he or she grows through childhood into adult life. There are a number of methods which have their advocates, including classical percussion and drainage, the forced expiration technique[7], autogenic drainage[8], positive end expiratory pressure[9] and a variety of exercise routines. In infants and very young children the percussion and drainage technique is used as they cannot co-operate with other forms of therapy. The precise regimen used in a particular case needs to be tailored to individuals' requirements, their compliance with treatment and the ability to perform the appropriate respiratory manoeuvres. The forced expiration and autogenic drainage techniques encourage independence. The positive pressure technique at the usual pressure of 10-14 cmH$_2$0 has been shown to benefit some but not all[10] and high pressures of 40-50 cmH$_2$0 may be helpful in patients with a great deal of airflow obstruction and volume dependent airway collapse[11]. Whichever technique is employed, it should be introduced by an experienced physiotherapist and assessed for its effectiveness.

Antibiotic Therapy
The natural history of sputum microbiology in CF begins with Staphylococcal infections in infancy and early life, through *Haemophilus influenzae* in mid-childhood and in many patients acquisition of *Pseudomonas aeruginosa* (PA), in combination with other organisms, in mid to late childhood and early adult life. Hence the antibiotic regimens need to take this into account as well as sputum results from individual patients. The common pattern of early *Staphylococcus aureus* colonisation has resulted in the widely held belief that anti-Staphylococcal "prophylaxis" may retard colonisation and subsequent lung damage. However evidence for the prophylactic approach rather than intermittent treatment as the required regimen is lacking. In the absence of clear benefit of continual prophylaxis against *S. aureus* it would at least seem prudent to treat infants and very young children who present with respiratory infections with continuous antibiotics for a period of 6-9 months and then go onto an intermittent regimen. The choice of antibiotic will be between flucloxacillin and erythromycin or possibly co-trimoxazole. The latter has some anti-staphylococcal action and is convenient on a twice daily regimen. It is also effective against *Haemophilus influenzae* which are not uncommon in the older infant and very young child. Broad spectrum penicillins are also popular in the very young child, particularly if no pathogens are consistently isolated. Usually in later childhood, PA begins to colonise the respiratory tract, and the debate between intermittent symptomatic versus more elective treatment still rages. Both these issues of chronic versus intermittent antibiotic regimens need to be set against a background of a continually improving prognosis found in all major centres regardless of antibiotic policy.

It should be remembered in patients with PA that because of the often exuberant growth of this organism, other pathogens, particular *Haemophilus influenzae,* may not be easily cultured. Hence in patients who do not appear to respond to standard anti-Pseudomonal antibiotics, agents active against *Haemophilus influenzae,* such as co-trimoxazole or even chloramphenicol, should be considered. There is considerable debate concerning the significance of PA and its management. In much of the CF world, carers, patients and their families, PA has adopted a fearsome reputation. While there is no doubt that the presence of the organism is associated with moderate/severe lung disease and increasing evidence is accumulating that the host response to PA damages the lung (see section "The Future"), it is not clear whether antibiotics should be given prophylactically or on an intermittent as required basis. Evidence for a prophylatic approach with regular intravenous courses has come from a Danish CF Centre[12]. However this latter study used historical controls and, particularly in CF with a continually improving prognosis[1,2], such an approach will always favour later cohorts of patients. Opinion is fairly equally divided in major CF centres and until better prospective evidence becomes available it would seem reasonable to use an "as required" approached in those patients who are clinically stable, while using a more aggressive prophylactic approach in those with unstable disease and frequent exacerbations.

The choice of anti-Pseudomonas antibiotics is now large and remains one of personal preference and suitability for the patient (Figure 3). It is usual to administer 2 agents, one of which should be an aminoglycoside. A course of 10-14 days is usually sufficient and response is gauged by subjective assessment by the patient and by objective features such as reducing sputum volume, weight gain and improving lung function. Not all acute exacerbations will require intravenous courses, and the quinolone ciprofloxacin has proved to be of considerable value in the treatment of PA exacerbations although there have been concerns about its use in children because of it deposition in growing cartilage. There is now a great deal of experience of its use in young patients and most centres use the drug for intermittent courses without major problems. There are, however, concerns about its long term use and the emergence of resistance strains of PA[13].

Should all courses of intravenous antibiotics be given in a hospital setting? The answer must be no, but careful consideration needs to be given to the relative advantages and disadvantages of home therapy. When families are carefully selected and appropriate support is given, the results can be at least as good as those obtained in hospital and arguably better[14]. However not all families can cope with the added responsibility, and it must be remembered that treatment of exacerbations does not just involve antibiotics but also intensive physiotherapy and nutritional support. It may also be desirable to relieve the burden of intensive treatment from the family, particularly if other commitments compete for the substantial time required to perform home treatment effectively.

AMINOGLYCOSIDES	CEPHALOSPORINS	PENICILLINS
Gentamicin	Ceftazidime	Azlocillin
Tobramycin		Piperacillin
Amikacin		Ticarcillin
Netilmicin		

THIENAMYCINS	MONOBACTAMS	QUINOLONES
Imipenin	Aztreonam	Ciprofloxacin

Figure 3. Antipseudomonal antibiotics.

Aspergillus is often cultured from the sputum of patients who are colonised with PA, and does not require additional treatment unless associated with allergic bronchopulmonary aspergillosis, first described in 1967[15]. Classical symptoms and signs of this syndrome include a low grade swinging pyrexia, a high eosinophil count in peripheral blood, early and late skin prick test responses, strong precipitation lines to Aspergillus from serum and flitting areas of consolidation on the chest x-ray.

Intermittent positive pressure ventilation should be reserved for those infants presenting with a bronchiolitis-type illness and without severe lung damage[16]. There is considerable debate about the suitability of ventilator treatment in older patients with very severe lung disease, but this invariably has a very poor short term prognosis and is best avoided[17]. The exception would be those with moderately severe disease undergoing operative procedures for other conditions in whom some post-operative ventilation may be required, in the knowledge that support will only be required in the short term. The same principles should be extended to those very severe patients awaiting transplantation, since donor organs are in short supply and the waiting period often extends to months rather than days or weeks.

The Future

It is likely that improvements in survival will continue even with existing treatment regimens but with the isolation of the gene and gene product[18] and a much clearer knowledge of the basic defect, new and exciting treatments are on the horizon and some have already arrived. Modifying electrolyte transfer across the respiratory mucosa with agents such as amiloride has shown promise in a pilot study[19] and long term multicentre results are awaited. Modifying the inflammatory response of the host is also an area of considerable interest. An initial report demonstrating the effects of oral steroids used over a 4 year period showed a slower rate of decline in treated patients[20]. However, steroids have serious side effects and the use of non-steroidal anti-inflammatory drugs such as ibuprofen, methotrexate and possibly cyclosporin are being investigated. Current clinical practice is to use modest doses of steroids (up to 1 mg/kg daily) and attempt to wean patients who benefit onto an alternate day regimen with high dose inhaled steroids.

The anti-inflammatory treatment of CF is built around the observation that much of the lung damage due to chronic sepsis is the result of a heightened immune response, with recruitment of neutrophils into the lung and accompanying release of proteases including neutrophil elastases. These products are likely to damage the lung in themselves, and improved methods of controlling the florid immune response and the release of potentially toxic products are under active investigation at present. Recent reviews discuss this area in greater detail[21,22]. The isolation of the gene, and the replacement of the CF gene with normal genetic material in cystic fibrosis cells in culture, have opened the possibility of this line of thrapy, but many problems need to be overcome before this approach becomes a reality[23].

42

CONCLUSION

Cystic fibrosis remains a serious threat to life but it is now commonplace to expect most children to survive into adult life, and have a reasonably normal level of activity and attainment during their childhood years. Mortality has been largely exported into the adult age group and this has presented many chest physicians with a growing problem and challenge. Children presenting with CF for the first time in this present decade can look forward to improved life expectancy, and the possibility of a cure or at least a much better control of the lung component of this disease.

REFERENCES

1 Geddes DM, Dodge JA. Improving prognosis for cystic fibrosis in the UK. 1977-1985. *Thorax* 1988; **43**: 838.

2 Britton JR. Effects of social class, sex and region of residence on age at death from cystic fibrosis. *Br Med J* 1989; **298**: 483-487.

3 Wilcken B, Chalmers G. Reduced morbidity in patients with cystic fibrosis detected by neonatal screening. *Lancet* 1985; **ii**: 1319-1321.

4 Chatfield S, Owen G, Ryley HC, Williams J, Alfaham M, Goodchild MC, Weller P. Neonatal screening for cystic fibrosis in Wales and the West Midlands: clinical assessment after five years of screening. *Arch Dis Child* 1990; **66**: 29-33.

5 Mearns MB, Hodson CJ, Jackson ADM, Hanworth EM, Holmes Sellers T, Sturridge M, France NE, Reid L. Pulmonary resection in cystic fibrosis: results in 23 cases, 1957-1970. *Arch Dis Child* 1972; **47**: 499-508.

6 Whitehead B, Helms P, Goodwin M, Martin I, Scott JP, Smyth RL, Higenbottam TW, Wallwork J, Elliott M, de Leval M. Heart-lung transplantation for cystic fibrosis I: Assessment. *Arch Dis Child* 1991; in press.

7 Pryor JA, Webber BA, Hodson ME, Batten JC. Evaluation of the forced expiration technique as an adjunct to postural drainage in the treatment of cystic fibrosis. *Br Med J* 1979; **2**: 417-418.

8 Chevailler J. Autogenic drainage. In: *Cystic Fibrosis - Horizons*. D Lawson (Ed). John Wiley, Chichester 1984; p235

9 Falk M, Kelstrup M, Andersen JB, Kinoshita T, Falk P, Stovring S, Gothgen I. Improving the ketchup bottle method with positive expiratory pressure, PEP. A controlled study in patients with cystic fibrosis. *Eur J Respir Dis* 1984; 57-66.

10 Tyrrell JC, Hiller EJ, Martin J. Face mask physiotherapy in cystic fibrosis. *Arch Dis Child* 1986; **61**: 598-611.

11 Oberwaldner B, Evans JC, Zach MS. Forced expirations against a variable resistance: A new chest physiotherapy method in cystic fibrosis. *Pediatr Pulmonol* 1986; **2**: 358-367.

12 Szaff M, Hoiby N, Flensborg E W. Fequent antibiotic therapy improves survival of cystic fibrosis patients with chronic *Pseudomonas aeruginosa* infection. *Acta Pediatr Scand* 1983; **72:** 651-657.

13 Grerier B. Use of the new quinolones in cystic fibrosis. *Rev Infect Dis* 1989; **11** (suppl 5): 1245-1252.

14 Gilbert J, Robinson T, Littlewood J M. Home intravenous antibiotic treatment in cystic fibrosis. *Arch Dis Child* 1988; **63:** 512-517.

15 Mearns M, Longbottom J, Batten J. Precipitating antibiotics to *Aspergillus fumigatus* in cystic fibrosis. *Lancet* 1967; **i:** 538-539.

16 Dinwiddie R. Good outcome after prolonged ventilation in an infant with cystic fibrosis. *J Roy Soc Med* 1989; **82** (suppl 16): 44-46.

17 Farrell P M, Fost N C. Long-term mechanical ventilation in pediatric respiratory failure; Medical and ethical considerations. *Am Rev Respir Dis* 1989; **140:** S36-S40.

18 Rich DP, Anderson MP, Gregory RJ *et al.* Expession of cystic fibrosis transmembrane conductance regulator corrects defective chloride channel regulation in cystic fibrosis airway epithelial cells. *Nature* 1990; **247:** 358-363.

19 Knowles MR, Church NL, Waltner WE, Yankaskas JR, Gilligan P, King M, Edward LJ, Helms RW, Boucher RC. A pilot study of aerosolized amiloride for the treatment of lung disease in cystic fibrosis. *N Engl J Med* 1990; **322:** 1189-1194.

20 Auerbach HS, Williams M, Kirkpatrick JA, Colten HR. Alternate-day prednisone reduces morbidity and improves pulmonary function in cystic fibrosis. *Lancet* 1985; 686-688.

21 Elborn JS, Shale DJ. Lung injury in cystic fibrosis. *Thorax* 1990; **45:** 970-973.

22 Zach MS. Lung disease in cystic fibrosis - an updated concept. *Pediatr Pulmonol* 1990; **8:** 188-202.

23 Cystic fibrosis: towards the ultimate therapy, slowly. *Lancet* 1990; **336:** 1224-1225.

DISCUSSION

Audience Following a study in the United States, the group concerned have now withdrawn high dose prednisone because of quite significant effects on growth.

Dr Helms That group treated patients with high dose oral steroids and presented a 7 year follow up. Many patients had developed steroidal side effects including cataracts and crush fractures of the vertebrae. We are more cautious, and use 1 mg/kg on alternate days. Many of us also use high dose inhaled steroids, although that has not been proven to produce the same benefit.

Audience Are there any studies using topical steroids?

Dr Helms I am not aware of any, but they really need to be done because if we take the asthma model, we should be able to replace systemic steroids with high dose topically active inhaled steroids, at least on alternate days. Many of us are using that approach anyway.

Audience What about inhaled alpha 1–antitrypsin?

Dr Helms That is a suggested treatment because it will reduce or counteract the proteases being produced from neutrophils. There is a lot of interest in this because there is a possibility of treating alpha 1–antitrypsin deficiency with intravenous replacement therapy and possibly inhaled replacement therapy too.

Audience Is there any evidence that long term nebulised antibiotics make any difference?

Dr Helms The Brompton group showed quite a few years ago that using nebulised antibiotics can reduce the number of hospital admissions in patients who are colonised and who have had a lot of courses of intravenous antibiotics and exacerbations. There is a multi centre study in progress in the United States at present looking at the long term use of inhaled antibiotics. Our practice in this country is based largely on Margaret Hodson's group, and her experience in the late 70s using this type of treatment in a properly controlled study showed that it does work. Therefore I think there is a role for it.

Audience Is there a role for bronchoscopy in the treatment of the young child?

Dr Helms The central European CF doctors like to do bronchoscopy. We have attempted to do it in children who had had lobectomies, and most of those had actually had attempts to reinflate the collapsed lobe or segment without success. The experience is anecdotal but I think it is unrewarding, and you are back to where you were, usually within a few months.

Audience What is the current view on using gene treatment?

Dr Helms Once we have the cystic fibrosis mouse it will be appropriate to initiate some trials and then move on to consenting adult patients and then children. I tell most of my interested patients that in five to ten years from now, we may be looking at gene replacement therapy for the lung.

Audience Would the patients make an immune response to gene therapy, and how many cells would you need to transplant?

Dr Helms There are many things to overcome. Cystic fibrosis cells in culture have reverted to normal function with transvection. The current development is to look at a vector such as the adeno virus, which has predilection for respiratory mucosa. The other approach would be to package up DNA in liposomes for example, and use it as a replacement therapy rather than a "fix it once and for all" treatment. When you look at what has happened with the identification of the CF gene, which really was not thought possible at one time, the pace of change is quite amazing, so I think there is a good chance that we will have some kind of therapy along those lines within that sort of time scale.

PROBLEMS OF THE YOUNG ADULT WITH CYSTIC FIBROSIS

A K Webb
Regional Adult Cystic Fibrosis Unit
Monsall Hospital, Manchester

INTRODUCTION

The aim of young adults with cystic fibrosis is to survive a lethal disease. As a result, patient motivation, combined with aggressive medical treatment, has increased survival but only into the third decade[1]. Improved survival has resulted from managing these patients in centres where care is multidisciplinary and cumulative experience has evolved into expertise[2]. Survival may depend upon the intensity of the treatment[3] or social class and region of residence[4]. However, as the disease progresses and the options for controlling pulmonary sepsis decline, treatment of chest disease becomes increasingly difficult. In addition to infection, other pulmonary complications such as pneumothorax, haemoptysis, cor pulmonale and disabling breathlessness become manifest.

Cystic Fibrosis is a multisystem disease and the extrathoracic medical problems increase with age. These include diabetes mellitus, vasculitis of the skin, arthritis, hepatobiliary and gastrointestinal disease. The medical problems of the adult are compounded by a clear perception of a limited lifespan resulting in psychological stress (needing sympathetic counselling). Compliance may be difficult with a complicated regimen of self care, and needs understanding reinforcement. This article dicusses the problems of the chest, the increasing number of extra thoracic complications which arise as the patient grows older, and the stress of trying to lead a normal life against a background of poor health.

CHEST PROBLEMS

Pulmonary Sepsis

The respiratory mucus of patients with cystic fibrosis becomes infected in early childhood with *Staphylococcus aureus* and by early adolescence with *Pseudomonas aeruginosa*; impossible to eradicate with antibiotics, overall treatment is palliative, and death due to inexorable pulmonary sepsis occurs in the majority of patients during the third decade of life. An aggressive approach to pulmonary sepsis should incorporate three monthly intravenous antibiotics, physiotherapy twice a day, regular exercise and the prescription of nebulised antibiotics. It is difficult to evaluate the long term efficacy of each of these modes of treatment. For instance although there are many publications comparing the relative values of intravenous antibiotics, these trials are conducted over a short period of time (months) and evaluate very crude parameters of response whereas the relentless progression of the lung disease extends over decades. Some centres practise a policy of treating when an infective exacerbation occurs, others treat prophylactically every three months. Although a three monthly antibiotic policy curbs pulmonary sepsis, a liberal antiobiotic policy has the disadvantages of being expensive in a financially cold climate, it may induce antibiotic resistance, and may interfere with normal social life. Of perhaps greater concern is the emergence in some centres of multiresistant *Pseudomonas aeruginosa* and its replacement by more difficult to treat organisms such as *Pseudomonas cepacia*[5]. This organism appears to be transmitted between patients. In some patients its acquisition is marked by a sharp clinical deterioration. Segregation of patients from each other is practised in Europe according to the organisms cultured from their sputum; practical problems such as lack of facilities in the N.H.S. have precluded this action until now, but as the problem increases some provision will have to be made.

Recent interest has focused on the exaggerated host responses to pulmonary sepsis in patients with CF[6]. The persistent inflammatory response produces progressive lung destruction which is only marginally attenuated by antibiotics. Validated measurements of this response are C reactive protein, tumour necrosis factor, neutrophil elastase complex, free radical markers, and the interleukins. Attention is being directed to modulating this damaging process and the role of steroids is still being evaluated[7]; however they readily induce diabetes in the adult and steroid dependence is a contraindication to heart lung transplantation (HLT). A recent preliminary publication has evaluated the use of nebulised alpha 1 antitrypsin in reducing the level of neutrophil elastase in the epithelial lining fluid of the bronchial lumen, and demonstrated its superiority over administration by the intravenous route[8].

Pneumothorax
A pneumothorax occurs in about 10% of the adult CF population and is associated with severe disease[9]. A small air leak in the hypoxic patient can result in severe respiratory failure and will need aspirating. A large leaking pneumothorax can be a difficult management problem. It is easier to perform physiotherapy following insertion of a drainage tube. The lung may be slow to re-expand and yet surgery should be avoided if consideration is being given for HLT. Practically it is better to persevere with prolonged medical management.

Haemoptysis
Small streaks of blood in the sputum are common, but occasionally haemoptysis can be profuse and life threatening. Management can be extremely difficult in the sick breathless patient. Aggressive management may include bronchoscopy and selective bronchial angiography with gel foam embolisation[10]. Bronchial artery

48

ligation or lobectomy have also been used. However specialised facilities and experience are not always readily available in a district hospital. We have successfully used infusions of vasopressin to control profuse haemoptysis[11]. However fluid retention can occur with this regimen and fluid balance must be monitored carefully.

Respiratory Failure and Oxygen Therapy
The management of cor pulmonale in cystic fibrosis is difficult. The electrocardiogram can show evidence of right ventricular hypertrophy several years prior to death. Evidence from sleep studies has shown that daytime hypoxia is mirrored by prolonged night-time hypoxia. Oxygen desaturation during progressive exercise testing may be a useful predictor of nightime desaturation[12]. It has been suggested that pulmonary hypertension may be delayed by the institution of night-time oxygen therapy but it is unlikely that young adults would accede to this proposal[13].

The management of acute respiratory failure with carbon dioxide retention may require the institution of respiratory stimulants such as dopram, but mechanical ventilation should not be considered unless there is an obvious reversible cause. If the patient is hypoxic and retaining carbon dioxide only 24% oxygen should be administered and the blood gases rechecked. If the patient requires oxygen at night and is retaining carbon dioxide then a 24% face mask rather than nasal cannulae should be employed and an overnight infusion of dopram will also be required to prevent a continuing rise of carbon dioxide. Oxygen is a lethal drug and its administration should be documented on the prescription sheet at the end of the bed. If the patient is awaiting a heart lung transplant some centres have employed positive nasal pressure ventilation to bridge the gap. The potential for HLT has raised the expectations of the patients and their families. When the patient becomes terminal medical management should be directed at ensuring a peaceful death; the family may request ventilation and publicity to find a donor. This can impose a considerable burden upon the medical team.

EXTRA THORACIC PROBLEMS
The main cause of death in cystic fibrosis is pulmonary sepsis, but nearly every organ in the body can be involved with varying degrees of severity. Exocrine pancreatic malfunction has been solved with the introduction of the newer pancreatic supplements Creon and Pancrease. However, these may not be sufficient to overcome the high energy requirements of the patients.

The majority of adults are small, thin and underweight. The progression of lung disease can accelerate this process, which can be modified by the introduction of nocturnal nasogastric feeding or the siting of a feeding gastrostomy. Choosing and making it acceptable to the patient can be difficult. Underweight patients being considered for HLT are considered a poor surgical risk and are probably the most suitable candidates for supplementary feeding.

Pancreatic endocrine function also deteriorates as the patients mature. Fifteen percent of our patients have developed diabetes mellitus. The majority are insulin dependent. It is important to screen the patients repeatedly as persistent hyperglycaemia can exacerbate the chest condition. Dehydration can make sputum thicker and physiotherapy impossible.

Abdominal pain is a common diagnostic problem. Duodenal ulcer and biliary colic may occur in the same patient. Adult meconium ileus equivalent (MIE) usually develops as a result of failure to take sufficient pancreatic supplements. Two patients have been referred to our unit having had a laparotomy for MIE. In the acute situation this disaster can be avoided medically with the introduction of oral and rectal gastrograffin or large volumes of oral electrolyte solution. The combination of a general anaesthetic, an abdominal operation and poor respiratory function can be lethal. Chronic intussusception has been well described and can be diagnosed by the typical "bulls eye" appearance on abdominal ultrasound[14].

Hepatobiliary problems can cause diagnostic difficulties but have assumed a greater importance recently since patients with evidence of overt biliary cirrhosis are excluded from having a heart lung transplant. Cholesterol gall stones can cause recurrent cholecystitis and if the patient is anaesthetically unfit for cholecystectomy they can be dissolved with synthetic bile salts[15]. Occasionally gallstones are intrahepatic and impossible to remove.

The basic defect in cystic fibrosis affects membranes lining the gastrointestinal, respiratory and biliary epithelium. Progressive damage to the biliary tree results in cirrhosis and portal hypertension. Sclerosis of bleeding varices may be life saving. Recently Gaskin et al[16] have described narrowing of the extra hepatic biliary tree and suggest this should be looked for in all patients with liver disease. However further publications have suggested that the narrowing reflects a diffuse process affecting both the intra and extra hepatic biliary tree[17,18].

Lifelong pulmonary sepsis results in persistent stimulation of the immune system. Subclasses of immunoglobulins and circulating immune complexes are elevated; cutaneous vasculitis occurs in about 5% of patients and there may be an associated or independent arthritis. Cerebral vasculitis has also been described as a rare event[19]. Treatment with high dose corticosteroids will usually produce complete resolution once the correct diagnosis has been made.

Social and Psychological Problems

The self care of the young adult incorporates an everyday regimen of physiotherapy, exercise, nebulised antibiotics, self administered oral medication, domiciliary intravenous antibiotics and a dietary intake of at least 2500 calories. The spur to achieving these imposing goals may be the realisation that average survival of one's peers is only into the third decade of life. Set against this background of self knowledge is a desire to lead a normal life, get married and have a family. However CF males are all sterile and although the women are fertile pregnancy can be hazardous, while looking after a child (soon to be motherless) becomes impossible during the terminal stages of the disease.

Practical problems may intrude upon normal living. It may be impossible to obtain life insurance or a mortgage, it may be difficult to work full time or indeed to get a job. It is a credit to the resilience of these patients that they do lead such normal lives; the majority of our patients are working or studying for higher education. Adults with cystic fibrosis can be found in the ranks of lawyers, doctors, pharmacists, teachers, labourers, factory workers and occasionally criminals.

It is not surprising that compliance with self care is not always optimum[20]. However the enforcement of a rigorous discipline may be self defeating and designing a mutually agreed plan of care for the patient often produces a satisfactory compromise. It is a characteristic of adults with CF that they do not perceive themselves to be severely afflicted with the disease. It usually comes as a profound shock when it is suggested they need referring for a heart lung transplant.

Patients' psychological problems are related to the fear of dying, which is reinforced when friends of a similar age group die and their own terminal phase becomes apparent. Experienced social workers are invaluable in providing support in these situations. This will involve the whole family, and after death there may be a prolonged grief reaction and some anger from the family directed at the unit for failing to prolong the life of the patient. True psychiatric problems are unusual and no greater than those occurring in the normal population.

Provision of Care

Delivering satisfactory care to the young adult is becoming increasingly difficult in the changing climate of the N.H.S. The recent publication from the Royal College of Physicians establishing the correct guidelines of care for adults with cystic fibrosis is timely[21]. However one doubts that it will have any practical effect. Regional Medical Officers are devolving medical care to the districts, and if a cystic fibrosis unit provides regional care it will have to be self financing by cross charging other districts for the very expensive costs of the patients. Fund holding practices may have only limited budgets for individual expensive patients and may be unwilling to refer them to centres. Our unit receives funding for essential staffing from charitable sources which should be provided by the N.H.S. While it is welcome, this funding is not permanent although its withdrawal would reduce satisfactory levels of patient care.

Future Problems

Genetecists have discovered the chromosomal defect, but because of the various genetic mutations have not improved the prospects of screening out the disease. Shortly cell biologists and biochemists will delineate the abnormal protein (Cystic Fibrosis Transmembrane Regulator). How to administer this to the adult patient remains a stupendous practical, medical and ethical dilemma. The excitement that heart lung transplantation produced is declining as it progresses from experimental to routine medical practice. However although it saves patients from inevitable death the paucity of donors means approximately 30% of patients die on the waiting list. This can place an intolerable strain on doctors, patients and families. Will xenografts produce an answer or just more problems?

REFERENCES

1   Corey M, McLaughin FJ, Williams M, Levison H. A comparison of survival, growth, and pulmonary function in patients with cystic fibrosis in Boston and Toronto. *J Clin Epidemiol* 1988; **41:** 583-591.2

2   Szaff M, Hoiby N, Flensborg E. Frequent antibiotic therapy improves survival of cystic fibrosis patients with chronic Pseudomonas aeruginosa. *Acta Pediatr Scand* 1983; **72:** 651-7.

3   Wood RE, Piazza F. Survival in cystic fibrosis: correlation with treatment in three cystic fibrosis centres. In: *10th International Cystic Fibrosis Conference,* edited by Mellis and Thompson. Amsterdam, Excerptica Medica 1988; 79-80.

4   Britton JR. Effects of social class, sex and region of residence on age at death from cystic fibrosis. *Br Med J* 1989; **298:** 483-7.

5   Thomassen MJ, Demko CA, Klinger JD, Stern RC. *Pseudomonas cepacia* colonisation among patients with cystic fibrosis. A new opportunist. *Am Rev Respir Dis* 1985; **131:** 791-6

6   Elborn JS, Shale D. Lung injury in cystic fibrosis. *Thorax* 1990; **45:** 970-3.

7   Auerbach HS, Williams M, Kirkpatrick JA, Colten HR. Alternate day prednisolone reduces morbidity and improves pulmonary function in cystic fibrosis. *Lancet* 1985; **11:** 686-8.

8   McElvaney NG, Hubbard RC, Birrer P, Chernick MS, Caplan DB, Frank MM, Crystal RG. Aerosol al-antitrypsin treatment for cystic fibrosis. *Lancet* 1991; **337:** 392-4.

9   Penketh A, Knight RK, Hodson ME, Batten JC. Management of pneumothorax in cystic fibrosis. *J Pediatr Surg* 1983; **18:** 492-7.

10 King AD, Cumberland DC, Brennan SR. Management of severe haemoptysis by bronchial artery embolisation in a patient with cystic fibrosis. *Thorax* 1989; **44:** 523-4.

11 Bilton D, Webb AK, Foster H, Mulvenna PM, Dodd M. Life threatening haemoptysis in cystic fibrosis: an alternative therapeutic approach. *Thorax* 1990; **45:** 975-976.

12 Veersteeg FGA, Bogard JM, Ratgeever JW *et al.* Relationship between airways obstruction, desaturation during exercise and nocturnal hypoxia in cystic fibrosis patients. *Eur Respir J* 1990; **3:** 68-73.

13 Gotz MH, Burghuber OC, Salzer-Muhar U, Woloscuk W, Weissel M, Hartter E. Cor pulmonale in cystic fibrosis. *J R Soc Med* 1989; **82:** Supp 16: 26-31.

14 Webb AK, Khan A. Chronic Intussusception in a young adult with cystic fibrosis. *J R Soc Med* 1989; **82**: Supp 16: 47-8.

15 Salh W, Howat J, Webb AK. Dissolution of gallstones with ursodeoxycholic acid in patients with cystic fibrosis. *Thorax* 1988; **43**: 490-91.

16 Gaskin KJ, Waters DLM, Howman-Giles R *et al*. Liver disease and common bile duct stenosis in cystic fibrosis. *New Engl J Med* 1988; **318**: 340-46.

17 Bilton D,Fox R, Webb Ak, Lawlor W, McMahon RFT, Howat JMT. Pathology of common bile duct stenosis in cystic fibrosis. *Gut* 1990; **31**: 236-38.

18 Nagel RA, Javaid A, Meire HB *et al*. Liver disease and bile duct abnormalities in adults with cystic fibrosis. *Lancet* 1989; **11**: 1422-25.

19 Finnegan MJ, Hinchcliffe J, Russell-Jones D, Neil S, Sheffield E, Jayne D, Wise A, Hodson ME. Vasculitis complicating cystic fibrosis. *Q J Med* 1989; **267**: 609-21.

20 Passero MA, Remor B, Salomoon J. Patient reported compliance with cystic fibrosis therapy. *Clin Pediatr* 1981; **20**: 264-68.

21 A report of the Royal College of Physicians. *Cystic Fibrosis in Adults: recommedations for care of patients in the UK*. The Royal College of Physicians of London, 1990.

DISCUSSION

Dr Phillips You said you have your patients in every three months for treatment with anti-pseudomonal antibiotics. Do you treat according to sensitivities or do you just use a routine one or a pair of antibiotics?

Dr Webb That is difficult to answer because you can grow 3 strains of Pseudomonas in one patient, on one culture with varying sensitivities. So we do treat according to sensitivities but we are aware of not always treating patients comprehensively. Bacteriology is a difficult problem to resolve in terms of sensitivities, but we monitor everything closely. We measure sputum weight every day as a response to antibiotics and therefore we review the patients every 3 or 4 days in terms of changes on antibiotics.

Audience Are you providing a Regional service for the adults?

Dr Webb Part of the reason for doing a cost analysis was that the Region did support us, but then informed us that we should be self sufficient and self continuing so yes we do provide a Regional service. We have 86% of the adults from the North West and the other 14% are scattered elsewhere. We get many referrals from the two large paediatric units at the age of 16.

Dr Phillips What is your approach to ventilating patients with end stage chronic respiratory failure who are on the heart lung transplant waiting list, and with the relatively recent advent of more effective means of non invasive ventilation do you see a role for that?

Dr Webb The answer to your first question is that as a result of our experience we have a mandatory policy not to ventilate anyone who has end stage lung disease unless there is an underlying easily reversible cause such as the inappropriate administration of sedatives. We have experienced the horror that it can cause in the wrong situation so we would never do it again, and I think that is the consensus feeling in the majority of practising physicians. Concerning the second point, we are certainly planning to use positive pressure nasal ventilation if patients are on the heart lung transplant list and we cannot control their CO_2 with things like doxapram. We have not done it so far but the Brompton Group and Barts have used it successfully for some time.

Dr Phillips I think you implied that the evidence for cross infection in CF is gaining ground. Do you foresee that all units with practice isolationist policies?

Dr Webb I agree this may be a worthwhile policy for *Pseudomonas aeruginosa* through the evidence is difficult to find. I think there may be further evidence for direct patient to patient transfer in the future but meanwhile we have taken no action. The adult patients tend to discuss it amongst themselves and practice segregation of their own volition. Some people feel it is very important, others not, but there is no policy in the UK.

Dr David The one thing that has happened here is that a UK cohort of patients were going to a CF camp. That was cancelled because of the worries about cross infection as a result of data from a camp in Canada where there were concerns expressed about the acquisition of *Pseudomonas cepacia* at the camp. There are a lot of difficulties with that data since it is quite clear that a lot of patients also acquire *Pseudomonas cepacia* without going to camps and without meeting other patients.

PHYSIOTHERAPY FOR CYSTIC FIBROSIS

Mary E. Dodd
Regional Adult Cystic Fibrosis Unit
Monsall Hospital, Manchester

INTRODUCTION

The progression of lung disease in cystic fibrosis (CF) is caused by purulent secretions blocking small airways. Chronic infection and hypersecretion lead to impaired mucociliary clearance, atelectasis and hyper-inflation. Destruction of the bronchial wall by proteolytic enzymes released from mucopurulent secretions causes airway instability[1]. Effective clearance of these secretions by physiotherapy techniques and control of the infection by the judicious use of antibiotics is vital to the respiratory management of CF.

As knowledge of the pulmonary pathophysiology of CF increases, the effective clearance of infected secretions presents a continuing challenge to even the most experienced physiotherapist. Survival into adult life is a reality for the majority of patients. The need for an effective, efficient and independent treatment has become imperative to meet the needs of today's demanding "normal" lifestyle. This paper discusses the application of physiotherapy techniques and adjuncts to fulfil these requirements. Techniques and adjuncts including autogenic drainage, positive expiratory pressure and the active cycle of breathing techniques[2] including the forced expiration technique (FET)[3] have been evaluated. For the majority of patients the active cycle of breathing techniques is sufficient to optimise sputum clearance, but for others, various adjuncts will be required to complement the technique in order to achieve the maximum effect.

The Active Cycle of Breathing Techniques

The active cycle of breathing techniques (Figure1) incorporates three essential components: breathing control, thoracic expansion exercises and the forced expiration technique. Collectively these techniques mobilise and remove secretions without increasing airways obstruction and lung function is improved[4].

Breathing control

Periods of breathing control using tidal volume breathing at the patient's own rate are interspersed between the other two components to prevent any increase in airways obstruction and to avoid fatigue. The length of time required by each individual varies with the degree of airways obstruction. Longer periods may be necessary in the short term during an acute infective exacerbation and in the long term as the airways obstruction increases due to progression of the disease.

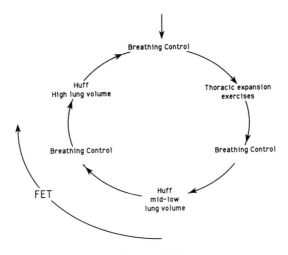

Figure 1. The active cycle of breathing techniques

Thoracic expansion exercises

Thoracic expansion exercises emphasising a slow deep inspiration to total lung capacity followed by a relaxed passive expiration form the component aimed at mobilising secretions. The increase in lung volume expands alveoli by the concept of interdependence[5] and opens the collateral airways to enable air to get behind trapped secretions[6] to reverse atelectasis. Three or four deep breaths are recommended, followed by a period of breathing control. Chest clapping is not essential[7] but many patients find this technique helpful. It should not be painful or prolonged and will not cause any deterioration in arterial oxygen saturation if combined with thoracic expansion exercises and breathing control[8]. Chest clapping stimulates coughing in babies and young children and is the technique used in gravity assisted positions to clear their secretions. Shakings and vibrations are techniques which may be used by the physiotherapist during the expiratory phase to enhance mobilisation of the secretions.

The forced expiration technique

Secretions can be mobilised and cleared from the airways using the forced expiration technique. It comprises a huff causing dynamic compression and narrowing of the airways, followed by a period of breathing control to relax the bronchial smooth muscle[9] and avoid bronchoconstriction. Its effect can be analysed by the concept of the equal pressure point (EPP). During a forced expiration a point is reached where the pressure in the airways equals the intrapleural pressure, the EPP. Compression and vibration occur downstream from this point. As the

56

forced expiration continues the lung volume decreases moving the EPPs and regions of compression upstream towards the alveoli. At lung volumes above functional residual capacity (FRC) the EPPs are located in the lobar or segmental bronchi, below FRC they move towards the alveoli[10]. A continuous huff from mid to low lung volume will therefore mobilise secretions in the more peripheral airways.

It has been suggested that coughing is the most effective method of clearing secretions[11,12] but it was not compared with the forced expiration technique. The mean transpulmonary pressure generated during coughing is greater than huffing [13] and clearance becomes inefficient as flow is limited. A huff or cough at a high lung volume will efficiently clear secretions from the upper airways.

The sequence of FET.
- one or two huffs from mid-low lung volume
- breathing control
- huff at high lung volume

The huff is produced by contraction of the abdominal muscles whilst the glottis remains open. It should be forceful but not violent. Expiratory flow volume curves in CF (Figure 2) suggest that for different patients the location and degree of airways obstruction varies. This has important implications for tailoring the technique for the individual patient. The rate of flow of the huff will be different

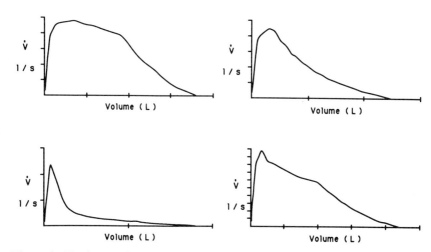

Figure 2. Expiratory flow volume curves in CF

for each individual varying with the degree of obstruction and progression of the disease[9]. Severity of lung dysfunction in CF is characterised by destruction of the bronchial wall, causing a decrease in bronchial muscle tone and airway instability[1]. Such over-compliant large airways dilate above normal during inspiration and collapse more readily during expiration, adding a downstream resistance to the upstream stenosis. Increased compression of central airways during a forced expiratory manoeuvre (huff or cough) prevents the EPP moving upstream, thereby increasing upstream resistance. This decreases peripheral expiratory airflow, reduces the efficacy of huffing and coughing and impairs expectoration[14]. The effectiveness of a forced expiration is determined by the flow and cross sectional area of the airway[10]. The huff can be varied to provide the fine balance of increasing flow without causing total collapse of the airways to ensure effective and efficient clearance of secretions.

Although the huff is different for each individual it is easy to learn and can be introduced to children from the age of two years. Assistance with the active cycle of breathing techniques is taught to parents and is required until the age of 8 or 9 years. Independence with the technique is then encouraged, initially under the watchful eye of parents and physiotherapist, until the child is competent. This period of supervision will allay any fear of ineffectiveness for the parent. However, assistance is still valued during times of increased breathlessness when self treatment may be tiring.

More sputum is expectorated when the active cycle of breathing techniques is performed in gravity assisted positions compared with sitting[15]. The areas of the lung requiring treatment will vary and are carefully assessed for each patient. The positions can be modified during an acute infective exacerbation if breathlessness is a presenting symptom. At work and school or during short holiday periods when gravity assisted positions may be inconvenient, the sitting position is a useful alternative. The active cycle of breathing techniques is repeated in each position until the huff or cough is no longer productive of sputum or the patient requires a rest.

The length and number of daily treatments will be different for each individual. Twenty to thirty minutes once or twice daily depending on sputum volume is sufficient to clear secretions and is acceptable for most patients when their condition is stable. Even if secretions are minimal or absent, a regular daily routine is recommended from the time of diagnosis. Compliance with chest physiotherapy in adolescence can be a problem[16]. Patients who are well disciplined in a daily regimen from an early age may find it easier to accept treatment at a later stage. During periods of increased sputum production it will be necessary to increase the number of treatments to four or five times a day. A realistic daily regimen is worked out between the physiotherapist and patient with consideration of life-style and disease severity.

Bronchodilator Therapy

Relief of bronchoconstriction with a consequent improvement in airway calibre will complement the active cycle of breathing techniques to enhance sputum clearance and decrease the work of breathing. Inhalation of both sympathomimetic and parasympathomimetic agents has been shown to reverse airways obstruction in CF[17], although the adult population appears to gain more benefit from anticholinergic drugs than children[18]. Reports of the bronchodilator response vary; some authors suggest that patients with poor lung function are more responsive[18], whilst others describe the opposite effect[19]. In a study by Hordvick et al[20] there was no significant difference between the two groups but the response was greater in winter than summer and varied during a course of therapy for a pulmonary infection. The response to bronchodilators, which was low on admission, improved during the course of intravenous therapy in correlation with increases in spirometry, but disappeared in certain patients when spirometric baselines reached their best.

Nebulised terbutaline inhaled prior to chest physiotherapy significantly increased sputum expectoration and radioaerosol clearance from the lung in patients with bronchiectasis[21]. The authors feel the mechanism was unclear but in agreement with Wood et al[22] it could possibly be explained by a combination of improved cilial beat frequency[23] and the increased airflow following the relief of bronchoconstriction.

A decrease in bronchial muscle tone causing airway instability has previously been described. Bronchodilator therapy will further decrease bronchomotor tone and increase collapsibility. Although this could result in impaired sputum expectoration, the improved conductance reduces the work of breathing. It is of interest that certain patients report considerable benefit from bronchodilator therapy following chest clearance.

Bronchodilator therapy prior to chest clearance reverses airways obstruction and improves mucociliary clearance for some patients but may cause a paradoxical deterioration in others. Initial assessment, re-evaluation during an infective exacerbation, and continual monitoring as the disease progresses, are essential to provide maximum benefit from this therapy.

Humidification Therapy

In comparison with other lung diseases the viscid tenacious sputum in CF has been shown to have a reduced water content[24]. The reason for this is defective electrolyte movement across the epithelial membrane, resulting in decreased sodium and chloride ion content in the secretions and impaired transfer of water to the airway lining fluid[25]. Dehydration of the periciliary layer increases sputum viscosity, decreases cilial activity and makes expectoration difficult. There is a lack of data to support the efficacy of humidification therapy. Sutton et al[21] reported improved sputum expectoration in bronchiectatics when chest physiotherapy was preceded by the inhalation of nebulised isotonic saline compared with physiotherapy alone. A possible explanation was rehydration of the pericilary layer improving cilial beat frequency which supports the value of humidifying the airway.

Humidification equipment producing a mist of nebulised particles falls into two categories; ultrasonic and jet nebulisers. To provide adequate humidification of small airways the aerosol must contain droplets with a mass median diameter of $<5\mu$. The ultrasonic nebulisers deliver a very dense mist, however induced bronchoconstriction occurs in many patients. Heat and an effecient jet nebuliser system to produce respirable particles are less irritating for these patients and for those who are wheezy. The mist is usually inhaled during chest clearance, to increase humidity to the airways at the time of expectoration.

Some patients with CF have hyper-reactive airways, and inhalation of cold aerosol or hypotonic and hypertonic solutions will have a bronchoconstricting effect. Isotonic normal saline (0.9%) is recommended for humidification therapy. Careful evaluation by measurement of PEFR or FEV 1 before and after inhalation of any solution from any device is essential.

Controlled oxygen therapy will require continuous high humidification. A humidity cuff which partially surrounds the venturi of the oxygen mask enables the entrained air to be humidified at low oxygen concentrations.

Mucolytics
Mucolytic drugs, eg. acetylcysteine, alter the rheological properties of sputum and reduce the viscosity, but are irritating and rarely used. The use of amiloride inhalations is a new approach to improving airway clearance[26]. It aims to block the excessive Na+ absorption of the epithelium and prevent dehydration of the respiratory secretions. Compared with normal saline, amiloride inhalations improve mucociliary clearance and cough clearance and reduce sputum viscosity [27]. However its action is of short duration (10-40 minutes) and inhalations are recommended 4 times daily.

Mechanical Aids
Mechanical aids are not advocated for routine use but can be a valuable adjunct when secretions are difficult to mobilise and removal by the usual methods is compromised by severe lung disease.

Intermittent positive pressure breathing (IPPB) increases tidal volume and expands the lung by applying a positive pressure to the airway during inspiration. This technique is particularly helpful when the patient is tired and exhausted, but an unnecessarily high pressure should be avoided because of the potential risk of a pneumothorax.

During periodic continuous positive airway pressure (PCPAP), a positive pressure is applied throughout inspiration and expiration. FRC is raised and collateral ventilation may be improved to areas of atelectasis without any increase in tidal volume. PCPAP has a limited use in CF but reduces the work of breathing. Pleuritic pain not easily controlled by analgesic drugs may be a problem during acute pulmonary infections. PCPAP may be of value when an increase in tidal volume would obviously increase the discomfort.

The positive expiratory pressure (PEP) mask is designed to increase peripheral airway pressure and avoid airway closure by expiring against an external resistance. Compared with the active cycle of breathing techniques PEP conferred no advantage in stable patients[28], but in the presence of airway instability a trial of PEP may be helpful[29].

Exercise

The cardiorespiratory benefits of exercise are well proven[30,31] but its contribution to chest clearance can be misleading. Some authors claim that conventional chest physiotherapy can be replaced by physical exercise[32,33]. The results were based on improvements in lung function following a training course of high intensity exercise when the chest physiotherapy was removed. Measurement of expectorated sputum weight can be used to monitor the effectiveness of physiotherapy techniques.

When a home exercise programme using bicycle ergometers was compared with the active cycle of breathing techniques more sputum was expectorated during physiotherapy[34]. It was concluded that exercise should be complementary to chest physiotherapy and not exclusive. Many patients would prefer exercise as an alternative method of chest clearance and for some, with minimal secretions, this has often been an acceptable arrangement with both physiotherapists and physicians. In a recent study comparing exercise, physiotherapy and the combination of both, it was shown that any treatment which involved physiotherapy produced more sputum than exercise alone. The same effect was seen in high and low sputum producers. Although exercise could shorten physiotherapy time it could not replace it[35].

Nebulised Antibiotic Therapy

Nebulised antibiotics are an accepted form of therapy for patients with severe and moderate disease[36,37]. However, drug intolerance can be an adverse effect for patients in both groups[38]. Although bronchodilators afford some protection, assessment of the bronchconstrictor response should be routine practice before prescription of the drug. Baseline spirometry is recorded after nebulised bronchodilators and chest clearance, which always precede the administration of nebulised antibiotics. Further readings are recorded immediately, and 15 and 30 minutes after nebulisation of antibiotics.

The efficacy of drug deposition in the lungs is influenced by the aerosol droplet size produced by the nebuliser compressor system[39]. Antibiotic solutions are viscous and require a powerful compressor with high flow and pressure characteristics (eg. 8 litres/minute at 25PSI) to produce an aerosol with a recommended droplet MMD of <5µ. Weaker compressors lengthen nebulisation time and may decrease compliance with the treatment. It may be necessary to vent the exhaled gas to the outside via a one way valve system if the antibiotic is foul smelling or sticky.

This is essential for use in hospital or at home if siblings are affected, to avoid dormant organisms becoming resistant to the antibiotic. Instruction in the care and maintenance of the nebulising system must be given.

Physiotherapy for CF is an individualised treatment regimen requiring regular comprehensive assessment, finely tuned to match the continuing changes in lung disease and lifestyle.

ACKNOWLEDGEMENTS
I wish to thank Miss J A Pryor, Miss B A Webber and Dr A K Webb for their help.

REFERENCES

1 Zach MS. Lung disease in cystic fibrosis - current concepts. Congress Abstracts, Excerpta Medica, Asia Pacific Congress Series, *10th Internationl Cystic Fibrosis Congress, Sydney, Australia,* 1988; 72-9.

2 Webber BA. The active cycle of breathing techniques. *Cystic Fibroisis News* 1990; Aug/Sept 10-11.

3 Pryor JA, Webber BA, Hodson ME, Batten JC. Evaluation of the forced expiration technique as an adjunct to postural drainage in treatment of cystic fibrosis. *Br Med J* 1979; **2:** 417-8.

4 Webber BA, Hofmeyr JL, Morgan MDL, Hodson ME. Effects of postural drainage incorporating the forced expiration technique on pulmonary function in cystic fibrosis. *Br J Dis Chest* 1986; **80:** 353-9.

5 Mead J, Takishima T, Leith D. Stress distribution in lungs: a model of pulmonary elasticity. *J Appl Physiol* 1970; **28:** 596.

6 Menkes HA, Britt J. Rationale for physical therapy. *Am Rev Respir Dis* 1980; **122** (suppl 2): 127-131.

7 Webber BA, Parker RA, Hofmeyr JL, Hodson ME. Evaluation of self percussion during postural drainage using the forced expiration technique. *Physiother Pract* 1985; **1:** 42-5.

8 Pryor JA, Webber BA, Hodson ME. The effect of chest physiotherapy on oxygen saturation in the treatment of cystic fibrosis. *Thorax* 1990; **45:**77.

9 Pryor JA. The forced expiration technique. In: Pryor Jennifer A, ed. *International perspectives in physical therapy - 7 Respiratory care.* Churchill Livingstone, Edinburgh 79-100.

10 Macklem PT. Physiology of cough. *Trans Am Broncho-Esophagol Ass* 1974; 150-7.

11 Rossman Cm, Waldes R, Sampson D, Newhouse MT. Effect of chest

physiotherapy on the removal of mucus in patients with cystic fibrosis. *Am Rev Respir Dis* 1982; **126:** 131-5.

12 De Boeck CH, Zinman R. Cough versus chest physiotherapy. *Am Rev Respir Dis* 1984; **129:** 182-4.

13 Langlands J. The dynamics of cough in health and in chronic bronchitis. *Thorax* 1967; 88-96.

14 Zach MS, Oberwaldner B, Forche G, Polgar G. Bronchodilators increase airway instability in cystic fibrosis. *Am Rev Respir Dis* 1985; **131:** 537- 543.

15 Sutton PP, Parker RA, Webber BA, Newman Sp, Garland N, Lopez-Vidriero MT, Pavia D, Clarke SW. Assessment of the forced expiration technique postural drainage and directed coughing in chest physiotherapy. *Eur J Respir Dis* 1983; **64:** 62-8.

16 Passero MA, Remor B, Salomon J. Patient-reported compliance with cystic fibrosis therapy. *Clin Paediatr* 1981; **20**(4)**:** 264-8.

17 Pitcher-Wilmott RW, Matthew DJ, Ingram D, Tyson SL. Improvement in lung function after nebulised salbutamol and ipratropium bromide in children with cystic fibrosis. *Proceedings in 11th Annual Meeting European Working Group on Cystic Fibrosis Belgium.* 1881; 251.

18 Weintraub SJ, Eschenbacher WL. The inhaled bronchodilators ipratropium bromide and metaproterenol in adults with cystic fibrosis. *Chest* 1989; **95:** 861-4.

19 Macfarlane PI, Heaf D. Changes in airflow obstruction and oxygen saturation in response to exercise and bronchodilators in cystic fibrosis. *Pediatr Pulmonol* 1990; **8:** 4-11.

20 Hordvick JL, Konig P, Morris D, Kreutz C, Barbero GJ. A longtitudinal study of bronchodilator responsiveness in cystic fibrosis. *Am Rev Respir Dis* 1985; **131:** 889-893.

21 Sutton PP, Gemmell HG, Innes N, Davidson J, Smith FW, Legge JS, Friend JAR. Use of nebulised saline and nebulised terbutaline as an adjunct to chest physiotherapy. *Thorax* 1988; **43:** 57-60.

22 Wood RE, Wanner A, Hirsch J, Farrell PM. Tracheal mucociliary transport in patients with cystic fibrosis and its stimulation by terbutaline. *Am Rev Respir Dis* 1975; **11:** 733-8.

23 Greenstone M, Cole PJ. Ciliary function in health and disease. *Br J Dis Chest* 1985; **79:** 9-26.

24 Matthews LW, Spector S, Lem J, Potter J. Studies on pulmonary secretions. I. The overall composition of pulmonary secretions from patients with cystic fibrosis, bronchiectasis and laryngectomy. *Am Rev Respir Dis* 1963; **88:** 199-204.

25 Knowles MR, Stutts MJ, Spock A, Fischer N, Gatzy JT, Boucher RC. Abnormal ion permeation through cystic fibrosis respiratory epithelium. *Science* 1983; 1067-69.

26 Knowles MR, Church NL, Waltner WE, Yankaskas JR, Gilligan PG, King M, Edwards LT, Helms RW, Boucher RC. A pilot study of aerolised amiloride for the treatment of lung disease in cystic fibrosis. *N Engl J Med* 1990; **322:** 1189-94.

27 App EM, King M, Helfesrieder R, Kohler D, Matthys H. Acute and long-term amiloride inhalation in cystic fibrosis lung disease. *Am Rev Respir Dis* 1990; **141:** 605-12.

28 Hofmeyr JL, Webber BA, Hodson ME. Evaluation of positive expiratory pressure as an adjunct to chest physiotherapy in the treatment of cystic fibrosis. *Thorax* 1986; **41:** 951-4.

29 Oberwaldner B, Evans JC, Zach MS. Forced expirations against a variable resistance; A new chest physiotherapy method in cystic fibrosis. *Pediatr Pulmonol* 1986; **2:** 358-67.

30 Orenstein DM, Franklin BA, Doershuk CF, Hellerstein HK, Germann KJ, Hovowitz JG, Stern RC. Exercise conditioning and cardiopulmonary fitness in cystic fibrosis. *Chest* 1981; **80:** 392-7.

31 Cropp GJ, Pullano TP, Cerny FJ, Nathanson IT. Exercise tolerance and cardiorespiratory adjustments at peak work capacity in cystic fibrosis. *Am Rev Respir Dis* 1982; **126:** 211-6.

32 Zach M, Oberwaldner B, Hausler F. Cystic fibrosis: physical exercise versus chest physiotherapy. *Arch Dis Child* 1982; **57:** 584-9.

33 Stangelle JK, Winnem M, Roaldsen K, DeWit S, Notgewitch JH, Nilsen BR. Young patients with cystic fibrosis; attitude toward physical activity and influence on physical fitness and spirometric values of a 2-week training course. *International Journal of Sports Medicine* 1988; **9:** 25-31.

34 Sahl W, Bilton D, Dodd M, Webb AK. The effect of exercise and physiotherapy in aiding sputum expectoration in adults with cystic fibrosis. *Thorax* 1989; **44:** 1006-8.

35 Bilton D, Dodd M, Webb AK. The benefits of exercise combined with physiotherapy in cystic fibrosis. *4th Annual North American International CF Conference Pediatr Pulmonol Supp* 1990; Supp 5, 253-4 (A238).

36 Hodson ME, Penketh ARL, Batten JC. Aerosol carbenicillin and gentamicin treatment of *Pseudomonas aeruginosa* infection in patients with cystic fibrosis. *Lancet* 1981; **11:** 1137-9.

37 Littlewood JM, Miller MG, Ghoneim AT, Ramsden Ch. Nebulised colomycin for early pseudomonas colonisation in cystic fibrosis. *Lancet* 1985; **i:** 865.

38 Maddison J, Dodd M, Webb AK. Nebulised colistin. Assessing tolerance and compliance. 17th European CF conference Copenhagen (in press).

39 Newman SP, Woodman G, Clarke SW. Deposition of carbenicillin aerosols in cystic fibrosis: effects of nebuliser system and breathing pattern. *Thorax* 1988; **43:** 318-22.

DISCUSSION

Audience Do you think making patients cough has a role?

Mrs Dodd Coughing should be productive, and the aim of a cough is to produce sputum. If they have to cough more than once to do this then you should be using the other techniques to move the secretions up the airways first. It is tiring to cough.

Audience Have you any experience of using hypertonic saline in trying to cure these secretions?

Mrs Dodd Yes, we have one or two patients who use 7% hypertonic saline. We recommend normal saline for all humidification treatments although we know that isotonic or hypertonic solutions can induce broncho-constriction in patients with hyperreactive airways. However as long as peak flows or spirometry are performed before and after inhalation, and there is no deterioration, and it is helpful to the patient, we would use it. Very few patients can actually do so.

Audience Have you tried combining it with salbutamol?

Mrs Dodd One patient who uses it does combine it with salbutamol.

Audience Do you use PEP masks?

Mrs Dodd We use PEP masks for a problem, usually airway closure. However, we do inherit patients from other centres and some come to us on PEP masks. I do not try to change them, but a lot of them do change when they are taught the active cycle of breathing techniques.

Audience Do you use PEP masks with or without postural drainage?

Mrs Dodd Both. Patients who come to us tend to use it in the sitting position but if we are using it for a problem such as retained secretions in a particular area, then I use it in postural drainage positions.

Audience If you have a patient who presents with severe haemoptysis do you withdraw any part of the physiotherapy?

Mrs Dodd If a patient presents with severe haemoptysis you immediately withdraw the percussion if it is in use. Positioning is very important too. Patients will often tell you where the haemoptysis is coming from, and so I would not then lie them with that lung dependent because that increases the perfusion to the lung underneath and cause the haemoptysis to recur. Avoid coughing, and huffing should be very gentle. It is a catch 22 situation where the secretions have to be cleared and there is also blood down there, but you do not want to cause recurrence of the haemoptysis.

Audience How much evidence is there that percussion achieves anything?

Mrs Dodd A study at the Brompton of percussion in patients who were clinically stable has shown that it does not offer any advantage, but patients often say that they find it helpful and it has not yet been proved to be harmful. If patients find it helpful, I do not see any reason to withdraw it, as long as the physiotherapist and the patient realise it is not the most important technique, it is probably the least important.

Dr David I think the physiotherapist actually provides a lot of support for a lot of patients, teaching them how to use inhalers, teaching them how to do lung function techniques, and the physio is a very keen member of the team, possibly more important than some of us doctors.

CYSTIC FIBROSIS HEART-LUNG TRANSPLANTATION

Dr Tim Higenbottam
Mr John Wallwork
Papworth Hospital, Cambridge

This paper will discuss some of our experiences over the last six years, as well as the experience of many other centres that have been performing lung transplantation to treat cystic fibrosis patients. This, we hope, will provide some insight into the problems incurred by lung transplantation generally, specifically heart-lung transplantation; and some of the special problems involved in the transplantation of patients with cystic fibrosis.

At the beginning of our programme it was decided to undertake heart lung transplant surgery in one patient with cystic fibrosis and then to wait one year to discover whether or not it was successful before offering such surgery to other patients[1]. We waited a year because of the concerns that the transplanted organs would get infected or that because of poor intestinal lipid absorption there would be many more complications such as rejection, if cystic fibrosis patients underwent transplant surgery. As a result of our first patient's courage, it was possible to offer lung transplantation to other cystic fibrosis sufferers. To illustrate the success of surgery in this patient, the forced expired volume in one second (FEV_1) rose progressively after surgery and is now running at about 120% of predicted. She is now probably the longest surviving patient with cystic fibrosis who has had a heart-lung transplant. But it is important to appreciate that all has not been successful. Patients, despite great courage, have died as a result of complications of transplantation surgery.

A history of lung transplant surgery

We have now undertaken 108 heart-lung transplants at Papworth, and 37 of these patients had cystic fibrosis. This is now the most common diagnostic group. Heart and lung transplant surgery entered clinical practice following the carefully controlled studies undertaken by Dr Bruce Reitz[2]. Clinically it was first used to treat patients with primary pulmonary hypertension and Eisenmenger's syndrome[2]. It was the success of the operation that led to an extension of its use to treat chronic lung diseases, including bronchiectasis[3]. At this point, at Papworth and Harefield Hospitals, the first patients with cystic fibrosis underwent this form of surgery. Single lung transplantation, where one lung alone is replaced, was successfully reintroduced by Joel Cooper in Toronto in 1985 to treat pulmonary fibrosis or cryptogenic fibrosing alveolitis[4]. Since then, a number of other sorts of conditions have been so treated, such as pulmonary hypertension, and corrected Eisenmenger's syndrome. Because of fears of infection of the transplanted lung, single lung transplantation is not considered suitable for cystic fibrosis patients.

Double lung transplantation, where the recipients keep their own hearts, has been favoured in the USA[5] and in France[6]. Lack of sufficient donors in North America for cardiac transplantation has led to this practice, and Dr Alec Patterson and Prof Noirclerk in Marseilles have pioneered this form of surgery, particularly for patients with cystic fibrosis. In the UK, Prof Magdi Yacoub developed the technique of transplanting the heart-lung transplant recipient's own heart to a further heart transplant patient. Professor Yacoub christened this procedure the "domino" operation and it has proved very successful. In fact it makes up about one third of all the heart donors in our Institute.

The international figures from 1985-1989 for single lung and double lung differ. Double lung transplantation is associated with a one year survival of around 50%, compared with over 60% for single lung transplants. This perhaps reflects technical problems with the initial surgical procedure. Now double lung transplantation is undertaken using bilateral bronchial anastomsis or by use of internal mammary artery to enable revascularization of the tracheal anastomosis. This may provide better survival results. In heart-lung transplantation, actuarial survival is internationally around 60%, but it should be emphasised that this reflects the overall figures for many centres, from those that perhaps only do one or two transplants per year to those that are perhaps transplanting up to 50-60 patients a year. At Papworth we have now achieved 78% one year actuarial survival and 55% of patients are alive at 5 years.

Complications of heart-lung transplantation (HLT)

Rejection and infection of the lungs are the main complications of HLT and the methods we have developed to manage these patients now either avoid the complications or enable prompt treatment. Prevention of these mainly occurs at the level of preservation of the donor organs. The ideal is for the lungs to work immediately after transplantation without evidence of injury. In 1984, we had to transport the donor to our hospital and perform the donor operation in an adjoining theatre to the recipient operation so the ischaemic time for the organ could be kept down to below 55 minutes. As can be appreciated, there are enormous ethical problems in doing this so from a series of animal studies we developed a technique for preserving the lung to extend the ischaemic time. The system involves an infusion of prostacyclin into the donor lung just before the cold perfusate of colloid or blood is added. With this technique the majority of lungs achieved ischaemic times of between 2 and 3 hours, some in excess of 4 hours. As a result the HLT operation is now comparable with our cardiac transplant procedures where again the donated organ can be kept ischaemic for up to 4 hours. Obviously this development removed the need to transfer the donor. The HLT block can be harvested at the donor's hospital[7]. By using the preservation technique, the majority of patients no longer require assisted ventilation after 24 hours. Now, of 108 patients who have received HLT, there have been only 3 primary organ failures where the lungs have failed to work. Patients who receive good, functioning lungs have a very smooth passage on the intensive care unit. On the day following surgery, ideally the patient is out of bed exercising on a set of peddles, often walking about by around 3 days. Other centres use alternative methods of preservation but when our vasodilator technique, using prostaglandin E_1 (PGE$_1$), was introduced by the Toronto group they were able to double their survival for single lung transplantation. Again it illustrates the importance of the initial graft function.

We developed the technique of transbronchial biopsy of the lung performed through a fibreoptic bronchoscope[8]. Bruce Whitehead and colleagues at Great Ormond Street Hospital developed this method in adults further for use in children. They used a rigid bronchoscope enabling the same procedures to be conducted in children under the age of 5[9]. Through the fibreoptic bronchoscope or rigid bronchoscope biopsy forceps are introduced and pushed out into the periphery of the lung using radiological screening to correctly position the forceps. We biopsy all the lobes (lingula taken as a separate lobe on the left side) taking three biopsies from each. Alligator forceps are used as they provide lung biopsies up to 4 mm in size. The importance of this is that it provides a biopsy that has the three main elements of lung; that is blood vessel, and some alveolar and bronchiolar epithe-lium. The three elements are essential in order to distinguish between infection and rejection. It is necessary to biopsy more than one lobe; for example if only the upper lobe were to be biopsied we would miss about 32% of rejection episodes. Using this technique of multiple biopsies form one lung it was possible to demonstrate that the process of rejection is a patchy process. I acknowledge some of the pioneering work of my pathology colleague, Dr Susan Stewart and also transplant fellow, Dr Colin Clelland, who worked with us as a pathologist. They have shown how to distinguish the infiltrate of acute rejection and have described the changes which occur with treatment[10,11,12]. Characteristically, there is a dense infiltrate of activated lymphocytes around small vessels which, using immunostaining, has been shown to be T cells which are mainly CD4 "helper" cells. On treatment with high dose cortico-steroids the blood vessel cellular infiltrate lessens, but often staining with haemosiderin is seen. This means that rejection is a vasculitic process which has injured the small blood vessel. Dr Stewart has now established simple means of distinguishing opportunistic lung infections from rejections by histology. With such clear-cut diagnostic techniques, treatment has been more correctly defined.

When should biopsy be undertaken? Patients often live miles from our hospital and when they develop symptoms such as cough they need a test to know whether or not to inform us. We have found that during episodes of rejection and infection, proven by biopsy, the FEV$_1$ falls. Also the diffusing capacity of the lung for carbon monoxide (DLCO) and the vital capacity (VC), together with total lung capacity (TLC) fall in value[13]. It looks as if the lungs become less compliant with these complications[13]. We therefore decided to give the patients their own "laboratory", a turbine spirometer. These are pocket devices, battery operated, that enable a patient to make a record of FEV_1 and VC every day and, uniquely for a transplanted organ, our patients can measure their graft function on a 24 hour basis. A 5% drop in the FEV_1 value is sufficient for the patient to 'phone us and come in for a biopsy[14]. We have been able to demonstrate that it was quite satisfactory for picking up most of the episodes of rejection and this has simplified life enormously for many of the patients.

As a result of close monitoring and the transbronchial biopsy technique, we have reduced strikingly the incidence of death from early infection. In the first 37 HLT patients we saw four deaths from cytomegaloviris (CMV) pneumonia. Since 1987, we have had no further deaths. In all early cases of CMV pneumonia, the infection was transmitted in the donor organs. Now where possible, our recipients who have negative serology for CMV only receive organs from serologically negative donors[15].

For herpes simplex virus (HSV) pneumonia, we have been able to avoid deaths because HSV pneumonia occurs within the first 3 months after transplantation and it occurs only in patients who were HSV serologically positive before surgery, which makes up about half of our patients. To avoid this complication, such patients receive prophylactic antiviral agents such as acyclovir during the first three months[16]. Bacterial pneumonias remain a problem but many of these are donor related again and careful selection of donor organs is mandatory. The lung biopsy technique has enabled a more systematic and scientific-based evaluation of HLT patients. Other centres, such as Stanford in California, have been able to show that with a biopsy protocol similar to ours there has been a striking improvement in survival of patients after HLT. A major late complication of HLT is the development of severely disabling irreversible airflow obstruction. This condition has been shown to result from an obliterative bronchiolitis (OB). From a review of over 500 biopsies by Dr Colin Clelland, a relationship between lung function, namely a falling FEV_1, and the histological finding of airway fibrosis in association with vascular sclerosis was observed. Repeated and persistent episodes of rejection lead to those fibrotic processes[17]. Patients who achieve a value of FEV_1 greater than 80% by 6 months post-operation have a very low chance of developing these specific fibrotic changes in their biopsies. Furthermore, they have a low risk of dying over the next 2 years. By contrast, if the FEV_1 is below 40% at 6 months most will die from OB. The only treatment is to prevent OB developing by completely clearing each rejection episode.

Specific problems of HLT in cystic fibrosis patients
Cyclosporin is the major immunosuppressive treatment and as a result of its lipophillic character is poorly absorbed by CF patients. Detailed pharmacological studies performed by Andrew Trull of the Departments of Clinical Pharmacology

and Biochemistry at Cambridge have shown that the absorption is less in CF patients than non-CF patients. By taking the drug more frequently, however, we have managed to reduce the daily oral dose in the CF patient. This achieves adequate immunosuppression and reduces the cost. Meconium ileus equivalent occurs in CF patients after HLT surgery. This may reflect a background of constipation in severely sick CF patients awaiting transplant surgery. Perhaps it can be avoided by ensuring normal bowel function before the patients go for surgery. Nasal polyposis is really quite common in CF. A few of our CF patients have required maxillary sinus drainage procedures after HLT. Respiratory tract infections are a major concern in CF patients after HLT[18]. The HLT procedure leaves the recipient's own trachea which can be anticipated to cause problems. Alison Wood, a Ph.D student in our laboratory is studying chloride epithelial cell chloride channels, and has showed that the high mucosal potential difference (PD) of cystic fibrosis, mediating impaired regulation of chloride ion secretion and enhanced sodium absorption, remains in the recipient's own trachea although the transplanted lung has a normal mucosal PD[19]. The characteristic high CF potential difference is seen in the trachea down to the suture line while below the suture line relatively normal values of potential difference are found in the lung transplant patients. Whilst CF will not return to the lung transplant itself, infections from the trachea could pose problems after HLT. In our own group the prevalence of infection was no greater in the CF patients than the non-CF patients. Indeed, the infection rates in both groups follow the pattern of acute rejection. The more frequently rejection is treated the more often infection occurs. There seems therefore to be a close link between treatment for acute rejection and the subsequent problem infections.

What patients should be considered for HLT?
The indications for HLT in cystic fibrosis can be simply summarised. An FEV_1 of less than 25% of the predicted value, an elevated arterial $PaCO_2$ level and a fall in arterial oxygen saturation during a 12 minute walk exercise test. Contra-indications for heart and lung transplantation in CF are limited; mycetoma of *Aspergillus fumigatus* is the major one because the mycetoma commonly affects the pleural surface of the lung. We cannot be sure that surgery will remove fully the Aspergillus infection from the thorax. Pleurectomy and pleurodesis are relative contra-indications but we have done one transplant in a patient who has had a pleurectomy. Heart-lung transplantation alone is not considered for those patients with severe liver disease, but heart-lung and liver transplantation is offered to such patients.

In the summer of 1990, 64 patients with cystic fibrosis had been assessed. We considered the actuarial survival of both patients who had received HLT and those patients who had not. Using Cox's model, Dr Lynda Sharples has shown that after adjusting for severity of disease, i.e. $PaCO_2$, minimal oxygen saturation and FEV_1 % predicted, there was no improvement. We are just beginning to see a benefit in terms of survival but it is only at a 10% level. However, quality of life is greatly improved. This is associated with near normal lung function achieved by CF patients after surgery.

Limitations to HLT for CF
For patients from 5 to 49 years old, there are some 18 deaths per million per year from CF. Currently the actual number of donors for HLT available in the UK is about 5 per million per year. This means that for all the people who could conceivably be helped by this form of treatment, we are probably only going to be able to treat one quarter of them. Indeed a third of our patients on the waiting list died before surgery is possible. Although donor referrals may be increased it will not be until xenografting is available, that is using animal organs instead of human organs, that this limiting factor for HLT will be fully removed. This represents a major new development with far reaching ethical and cost implications.

ACKNOWLEDGEMENTS
We are indebted to the Cystic Fibrosis Research Trust for their continued support for our research.

REFERENCES
1 Jones K, Higenbottam TW, Walwork J. Successful heart-lung transplantation for cystic fibrosis. *Chest* 1988; **93:** 644-645.
2 Reitz BA, Wallwork JL, Hunt SA *et al.* Heart-lung transplantation:successful therapy for patients with pulmonary vascular disease. *N Engl J Med* 1981; **306:** 557-564.
3 Penketh AL, Higenbottam TW, Hakim M, Wallwork J. Heart-lung transplantation in patients with end stage lung disease. *Br Med J* 1987; **295:** 211-313.
4 Toronto Lung Transplant Group. Unilateral lung transplantation for pulmonary fibrosis. *N Engl J Med* 1986; **314:** 1140-1145.
5 Cooper JD, Patterson GA, Grossman R, Maurer J *et al.* Double lung transplant for chronic obstructive lung disease. *Am Rev Respir Dis* 1989; **139:** 303-307.
6 Noirclerc MJ, Matras D, Valliant A *et al.* Bilateral bronchial anastomoses in double and heart-lung transplantation. *Eur J Cardiothorac Surg* 1990; **4:** 314-317.
7 Hakim M, Higenbottam TW, Bethune D *et al.* Selection and procurement of combined heart-lung grafts for transplantation. *J Thorac Cardiovasc Surg* 1988; **98:** 474-479.
8 Higenbottam TW, Stewart S, Penketh AL, Wallwork J. Transbronchial lung biopsy for the diagnosis of rejection in heart-lung transplant patients. *Transplantation* 1988; **46:** 532-40.

9   Scott JP, Higenbottam TW, Smyth RL *et al.* Transbronchial biopsies in children after heart-lung transplantation. *Pediatrics* 1990; **86:** 698-702.

10 Hutter JA, Stewart S, Higenbottam TW, Wallwork J. Histological changes in heart-lung transplant recipients during rejection episodes and at routine biopsy. *J Heart Transplant* 1988; **7:** 440-444.

11 Clelland C, Higenbottam TW, Otulana B *et al.* Histological prognostic indicators for the lung allografts of heart-lung transplant. *J Heart Transplant* 1990; **9:** 177-186.

12 Celland C, Higenbottam TW, Scott JP, Wallwork J. The histological changes in transbronchial biopsy after treatment of acute lung rejection in heart-lung transplants. *J Pathol* 1990; **161:** 105-112.

13 Otulana BA, Higenbottam TW, Scott JP *et al.* Lung function associated with histologically diagnosed acute lung rejection and pulmonary infection in heart-lung transplant patients. *Am Rev Respir Dis* 1990; **141:** 329-332.

14 Otulana BA, Higenbottam TW, Ferrari L *et al.* The use of home spirometry in detecting acute lung rejection and infection following heart-lung transplantation. *Chest* 1990; **99:** 352-357.

15 Hutter JA, Scott JP, Wreghitt T *et al.* The importance of cytomegalovirus in heart-lung transplant recipients. *Chest* 1989; **95:** 627-631.

16 Smyth RL, Higenbottam TW, Scott JP *et al.* Herpes simplex virus infections in heart-lung transplant recipients. *Transplantation* 1990; **49:** 735-739.

17 Scott JP, Higenbottam TW, Sharples L *et al.* Risk factors for obliterative bronchiolitis in heart-lung transplant recipients. *Transplantation* 1991; **51:** 813-817.

18 Fradet G, Smyth RL, Scott JP *et al.* Cystic fibrosis: a new challenge for cardiothoracic surgery. *Eur J Cardiothoracic Surg* 1990; **4:** 136-141.

19 Wood A, Higenbottam TW, Jackson M, Wallwork J. Airway mucosal bioelectrical potential differences in cystic fibrosis after lung transplant-tion. *Am Rev Respir Dis* 1989; **140:** 1645-1649.

DISCUSSION

Audience I think I am right in saying that the risk of rejection decreases with time. Presumably the risk of developing obliterative bronchiolitis also decreases with time.

Dr Higenbottom Yes. If you can achieve normal lung function by six months then your chances of dying from obliterative bronchiolitis are zero. If you have reduced lung function below 30% at six months then your chance of dying of obliterative bronchiolitis is about 40%. This fits with our idea that it is really a rejection driven process.

Audience Is a transplant contraindicated in patients with mycobacterial infection?

Dr Higenbottam I think it must be treated prior to surgery. We have not transplanted anybody who had a mycobacterial infection. We advise people to eradicate it before they refer, as for other forms of transplantation. This standard approach has led us to have no tuberculosis in patients afterwards.

Dr Phillips Provided you detect obliterative bronchiolitis soon enough, how successfully can you treat it with immunosuppressives and steroids?

Dr Higenbottam I do not believe you can. Once an active fibrotic process has begun the patient is doomed and I would argue that at that point you pull back the augmented immunosuppression to avoid death through super-added infection. That has been quite a successful policy over the last year. Histological data shows the principal changes are fibrotic, and biochemical studies show very high levels of hyaluronic acid in the lavage of patients developing this rapid decline in function.

Audience How often can CF patients be subjected to transplant and lung biopsy in terms of quality of life?

Dr Higenbottam Two years ago they were having biopsies done at least every three months, but now there are very few having more than two biopsies done in the immediate post operative period, except those that have a lot of complications which make up about 15% of patients. We have actually pulled out of intense medical care of these patients to a remarkable degree because we have learned what the major complications are.

Dr Phillips Have you any thoughts on why heart lung transplant recipients reject their lungs but hardly ever reject their hearts?

Dr Higenbottam I suspect that looking at it in very simple terms there is an enormous endothelial surface in the lung, which is probably the major source of the antigen that the lung decides to recognise. In other words you are just draining all the activated lymphocytes into the lung.

LIST OF DELEGATES

Dr J Black
London

Ms N Beaumont
Cambridge

Ms J Henwood
Bury St Edmunds

Dr G Russell
Aberdeen

Dr R M Buchdahl
Uxbridge

D J P McClure
Ayre

Dr M J Wilkinson
London

Dr W J Bolsover
London

Mrs J Campbell
Kingston upon Thames

Ms J Sears
London

Dr B R Silk
Kettering

Dr R A F Bell
Banbury

Dr A G Thomas
London

Dr G M Wilson
Dewsbury

Dr I G Hodges
Mid Glamorgan

Dr P Husband
London

Dr J Challener
Huntingdon

Dr V Nerminathan
Leigh on Sea

Dr R Williams
Bath

Dr Ma Myo Aye
Merthyr Tydfil

Ms A E Murphy
London

Mrs A Kerridge
London

Ms R Jarvis
Barking

Miss S Lock
London

Ms M Kenny
London

Dr S Shekhar
Pontypridd

Dr M G MacMillan
Fife

Dr D'Costa Selwyn
Gravesend

Ms A Jean-Baptiste
London

Dr A Hutchings
London

Dr E Carter
London

Dr J E B Aitken
Aberdeenshire

Ms G Harper
Yeovil

Dr G J Roberts
London

Dr P Greally
London

Dr D M Isherwood
Liverpool

Dr D A Woolf
London

Dr S Meller
Carshalton

Dr J Bowell
Crawley

Miss G Braid
London

Dr E Waring
Worthing

Mrs M Cant
Glemsford

Dr M Raman
Birmingham

Mrs J Rutherford
Sudbury

Mrs N Congdon
Sudbury

Dr A Cook
London

Ms M Howell
Stonehouse

Ms J M Parrott
Stonehouse

Dr D T Hindley
Huddersfield

Dr P E Carter
Cumbria

Dr H M Fleet
HighWycombe

Dr R C Dias
Cleveland

Ms C E Harvey
Carshalton

Dr S P Babbington
Riseley

Dr C Brain
Hackney

Dr R Wilson
Salisbury

Dr O Glynn
Reading

Ms C M Taylor
Shrewsbury

Ms P Hart
Shrewsbury

Dr Q Mok
London

Dr E Hadjimamas
London

Dr S Poole
London

Dr M Leigh
Bedford

Dr L Grain
Winchester

Dr D A Sitaras
London

Dr C N Hill
Southampton

Dr T H J Matthews
Loughton

Mrs E M Ward
London

Ms A Robertson
London

Ms R Sury
London

Dr N M Croft
Edinburgh

Ms N S Cooper
Teddington

Ms M G Bond
Horsham

Ms L Parsons
Reigate

Dr S T Jones
Wakefield

Dr R Prosser
Newport

Ms F J White
London

Ms L Johnson
London

Dr E Abrahamson
Watford

Ms S Young
Edinburgh

Ms J Omambala
London

Ms F Ashworth
London

Dr D Barter
Kings Lynn

Dr M Kabole
Gloucester

Dr A C Elias-Jones
Nottingham

Ms K Herring
London

Dr I M Thakur
Chelmsford

Dr T K R Chandran
Crewe

Dr A Duthie
Nottingham

Dr S De Haan
Leicester

Dr E G Bos
Chatham

Ms K O'Donnell
London

Ms J Williams
Cheltenham

Dr M Elsawi
London

Dr K K Sawhney
Northampton

Dr P Day
London

Dr C K Horn
Leeds

Dr A J P Tometzki
Leeds

Dr K R Rao
Ipswich

Dr K Das
Rochford

Dr S Kotecha
London

Dr M R Thummala
London

Dr H Sharma
Cambridge

Dr B Alawar
London

Dr N Dawani
London

76

Dr J Farrugia
London

Dr B Olusanya
London

Dr S Shirole
London

Dr M Scott
Bromley

Dr M J Walshaw
Liverpool

Dr B Zoritch
Nottingham

Ms C Bentham
Middlesbrough

Dr M Scott
Bromley

Mrs H R Linford
Hull

Dr Massarano
Manchester

Miss C Bromley
Leicester

Dr K L Kenyon
Tadworth

Ms J A Wells
Scunthorpe

Ms J Fenn
Scunthorpe

Ms S Williams
Manchester

Ms J Hooper
Manchester

Mrs C Ireland
Romsey

Dr F G Hunt
London

Ms A Bowerman
Penarth

Dr A Thompson
Nuneaton

Dr F N Kokan
Westcliffe on Sea

Dr X Couroucli
Manchester

Dr T G Marshall
Edinburgh

Dr M F Urban
Lee

Mr M Harvey
Cambridge

Dr D J Kanabar
London

Ms J Algar
Scunthorpe

Dr G Phillips
London

Dr I Shellshear
Peterborough

Ms M Moran
Dublin

Miss S Thomas
London

Dr P Robert
Coventry

Ms L Duncan
Cheltenham

Dr M Sayer
London

Mr E A Agathos
London

Dr D Ross
Frimley

Dr K Ferguson
London

Dr K V K Rao
Rochford

Ms J A Morais
Cardiff

Dr T Ahmad
Newcastle upon Tyne

Dr S W Duwe
London

Ms D Rogers
Mid Glamorgan

Dr W A W Ismail
London

Mrs P M Jones
Chelmsford

Ms C A Lloyd-Jones
Clwyd

Dr Flynn
London

MEDICAL RELATIONS PUBLICATIONS

CURRENT APPROACHES SERIES

Endometrial Carcinoma
Risk/Benefits of Antidepressants
Childbirth as a Life Event
Sleep Disorders
Advances in Pancreatitis
Neuropsychiatric Aspects of Aids
Breaking Bad News
Mental Retardation
Panic - Symptom or Disorder?
Myocardial Infarction - Acute Care and Rehabilitation
Fibre - Is It Good For You?
Obsessive Compulsive Disorder
Hormone Replacement Therapy
Prediction and Treatment of Recurrent Depression
Research Methods in General Practice
Vertigo
Towards Confident Management of Irritable Bowel Syndrome
Suicide and Attempted Suicide - prediction, prevention
    and management

The above publications can be obtained by writing to:
DUPHAR MEDICAL RELATIONS
Duphar Laboratories Limited,
West End,
Southampton SO3 3JD